Language Arts

Arts

Grade 2

FlashKids™

Dear Parent,

This book was developed to help your child improve the language skills he or she needs to succeed. The book emphasizes skills in the key areas of:

- grammar
- punctuation
- vocabulary
- writing
- research

The more than 100 lessons included in the book provide many opportunities for your child to practice and apply important language and writing skills. These skills will help your child improve his or her communication abilities, excel in all academic areas, and increase his or her scores on standardized tests.

About the Book

The book is divided into six units:

- Parts of Speech
- Sentences
- Mechanics
- Vocabulary and Usage
- Writing
- Research Skills

Your child can work through each unit of the book, or you can pinpoint areas for extra practice.

Lessons have specific instructions and examples and are designed for your child to complete independently. Grammar lessons range from using nouns and verbs to constructing better sentences. Writing exercises range from the friendly letter to the research report. With this practice, your child will gain extra confidence as he or she works on daily school lessons or standardized tests.

A thorough answer key is also provided so you may check the quality of answers.

A Step toward Success

Practice may not always make perfect, but it is certainly a step in the right direction. The activities in this book are an excellent way to ensure greater success for your child.

Table of Contents

Nouns

> A **noun** is a word that names a person, place, or thing.
> The words <u>a</u>, <u>an</u>, and <u>the</u> are clues that show a noun is near.
> *Examples:*
>   a <u>man</u>, an <u>elephant</u>, the <u>yard</u>

DIRECTIONS Find the nouns, or naming words, below. Write the nouns on the lines.

apple	car	eat	hear	rug	bird	chair
girl	hot	tree	boy	desk	gone	over
truck	came	dirty	grass	pen	up	tiny

1. _____
2. _____
3. _____
4. _____

5. _____
6. _____
7. _____
8. _____

9. _____
10. _____
11. _____
12. _____

DIRECTIONS Circle the two nouns in each sentence.

13. The girl eats an apple.

14. A bird flies to the tree.

15. A chair is by the desk.

16. A boy sits in the chair.

17. The girl plays with a truck.

Practice with Nouns

Remember, a word that names a person or an animal is called a noun. A word that names a place or a thing is also called a noun.
Examples:
The <u>girl</u> and her <u>dog</u> sat on a <u>bench</u> in the <u>park</u>.

DIRECTIONS > **Circle the noun or nouns in each sentence. You should find eleven nouns in all.**

1. My sister plays in the park.

2. She rides in a car with our mother.

3. Sometimes our dog goes, too.

4. A boy feeds birds under the trees.

5. Let's go to the playground!

6. I see a cat under the slide.

DIRECTIONS > **Look at the nouns you circled. Decide if each noun names a person, a place, a thing, or an animal. Write the noun in the correct space in the chart below.**

Person	Place	Thing	Animal

Proper Nouns

A noun is a word that names a person, place, or thing. A **proper noun** is a word that names a special person, place, or thing. A proper noun begins with a capital letter.

Examples:
Noun	**Proper Noun**
girl	Kayla Stone
park	Yellowstone Park
bread	Tasty Bread

DIRECTIONS Find the proper nouns in the box. Write the proper nouns on the lines.

baseball	Bob's Bikes	Bridge Road	children
China	Elf Corn	Gabriel	Lindsey
man	New York City	Oregon	Pat Green
prince	robin	State Street	town

1. _____
2. _____
3. _____
4. _____
5. _____
6. _____
7. _____
8. _____
9. _____
10. _____

DIRECTIONS Circle the proper noun in each sentence.

11. I bought apples at Hill's Store.

12. The store is on Baker Street.

13. It is near Stone Library.

14. I gave an apple to Emily Fuller.

Practice with Proper Nouns

Remember, a proper noun is a word that names a special person, place, or thing. A proper noun begins with a capital letter.

DIRECTIONS Draw a line between each noun and its matching proper noun.

1. dog   Fastmart Grocery Store

2. park   Central Park

3. city   Chicago

4. woman   Ms. Ward

5. school   Lassie

6. store   Redbrook Elementary School

DIRECTIONS Rewrite each sentence by replacing the underlined noun with a proper noun.

7. <u>Teacher</u> gave us a lot of homework.

_____

8. Lucy loves to play with <u>cat</u>.

_____

9. Brady's best friend is <u>boy</u>.

_____

Names and Titles of People and Animals

The names of people and animals are proper nouns. The first and last names of a person or animal begin with a capital letter.

The titles of people begin with a capital letter. Most titles end with a period. These are titles of people:

Mr.   Mrs.   Ms.   Miss   Dr.

Examples:

Jack Sprat went to the airport.

Mrs. Sprat is looking for her dog Fluffy.

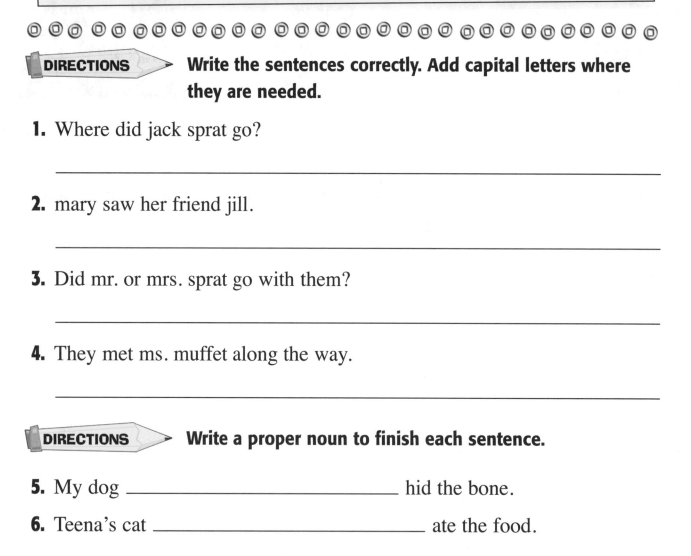

DIRECTIONS Write the sentences correctly. Add capital letters where they are needed.

1. Where did jack sprat go?

_____

2. mary saw her friend jill.

_____

3. Did mr. or mrs. sprat go with them?

_____

4. They met ms. muffet along the way.

_____

DIRECTIONS Write a proper noun to finish each sentence.

5. My dog _____ hid the bone.

6. Teena's cat _____ ate the food.

Practice with Names and Titles

Remember, the first and last names of people and animals are proper nouns. A proper noun begins with a capital letter. The titles of people also begin with a capital letter. These are titles of people:

Mr.   Mrs.   Ms.   Miss   Dr.

DIRECTIONS Underline the proper nouns in each sentence.

1. Meg and Tim walked to school.

2. They were going to help Ms. Lee before class.

3. On the way, they saw Holly Green.

4. Holly's dog Lucy followed them.

5. At school, Mr. Roberts laughed.

6. No dogs at school, Lucy!

DIRECTIONS Write two sentences about what Lucy will do next.

7. _____

_____

8. _____

_____

Names of Special Places

The names of special places are proper nouns. Cities, states, and the names of streets begin with a capital letter. The names of countries also begin with a capital letter.

Examples:

Jack saw his friends in <u>Miami</u>, <u>Florida</u>.

Their house is at 212 <u>Coconut Drive</u>.

I live in the <u>United States of America</u>.

DIRECTIONS ▷ **Write the sentences correctly. Add capital letters where they are needed.**

1. They walked along main street.

_____

2. My uncle drove through indiana and ohio.

_____

3. We went on a trip to mexico.

_____

DIRECTIONS ▷ **Write a proper noun to finish each sentence.**

4. The name of my state is _____.

5. The name of my town is _____.

6. The name of my street is _____.

7. The name of my school is _____.

8. _____ is a pretty place to see in our town.

Days of the Week, Months, and Holidays

The names of the days of the week are proper nouns. They begin with capital letters.

The names of the months are also proper nouns. They begin with capital letters.

The names of holidays are proper nouns, too. Each important word in the name of the holiday begins with a capital letter.

Examples:

The man flew in a spaceship on <u>Saturday</u>.

In <u>December,</u> he drives in the snow.

He had a picnic on the <u>Fourth of July</u>.

DIRECTIONS Complete each sentence. Use the words from the box. Find the day, month, or holiday that begins with the same letter as the underlined word.

Wednesday	Thanksgiving	Saturday	February	July

1. Francis Foley did not <u>walk</u> on _____.

2. He <u>flew</u> in _____.

3. Sometimes he <u>sails</u> on _____.

4. He <u>thinks</u> he will be home for _____.

DIRECTIONS Write a proper noun to complete each sentence.

5. My birthday is in _____.

6. My favorite day is _____.

7. My favorite holiday is _____.

Singular and Plural Nouns

A noun is a word that names a person, place, or thing.
A noun can tell about more than one person, place, or thing. Add <u>s</u> to most nouns to make them **plural nouns**, or "more than one."
Examples:

      One <u>girl</u> wears a black hat.

      Many <u>boys</u> wear funny masks.

DIRECTIONS Circle the correct noun to complete each sentence.

1. Two (boy, boys) went out on Halloween.

2. A (girl, girls) walked with them.

3. She wore a black (robe, robes).

4. There were two red (star, stars) on it.

5. It also had one orange (moon, moons).

6. The children walked up to a (house, houses).

7. Then, they knocked on the (door, doors).

8. Will they ask for some (treat, treats)?

9. Then, the children saw two (cat, cats).

10. Two (dog, dogs) ran down the street.

11. An (owl, owls) hooted in the darkness.

12. Many (star, stars) were in the sky.

13. The wind blew through all the (tree, trees).

14. The children clapped their (hand, hands).

15. Then, they sang a (song, songs).

Plural Nouns

Remember, add <u>s</u> to most nouns to make them name more than one.
Example:
    one <u>book</u>, four <u>books</u>

DIRECTIONS **Rewrite these nouns to make them name more than one.**

1. cap _____

2. chair _____

3. girl _____

4. tree _____

5. flag _____

6. boy _____

DIRECTIONS **Make the noun in ( ) mean more than one. Write the plural noun to complete the sentence.**

7. I plant _____ in my garden.
                 (seed)

8. I want to grow _____.
                     (carrot)

9. I plant some _____, too.
                   (pea)

10. My _____ help me.
              (friend)

11. They want to plant _____, too.
                  (garden)

More Plural Nouns

Add <u>es</u> to nouns that end with <u>x</u>, <u>ss</u>, <u>ch</u>, or <u>sh</u> to make them name more than one.

Examples:

one <u>fox</u>, two <u>foxes</u>

one <u>class</u>, ten <u>classes</u>

one <u>branch</u>, five <u>branches</u>

one <u>bush</u>, six <u>bushes</u>

DIRECTIONS Rewrite these nouns to make them name more than one.

1. lunch _____

2. dress _____

3. glass _____

4. dish _____

5. box _____

6. watch _____

DIRECTIONS Make the noun in ( ) mean more than one. Write the plural noun to complete the sentence.

7. Two _____ walk to the park.
(fox)

8. They sit on two _____.
(bench)

9. Their seats are only _____ apart.
(inch)

10. Then, they take out paints and _____.
(brush)

11. They paint pictures of trucks and _____.
(bus)

12. They hope to paint the _____ near the park.
(church)

Irregular Plural Nouns

Some nouns change spelling to name more than one.
Examples:

man—men
woman—women
child—children
foot—feet
tooth—teeth

DIRECTIONS Circle the correct noun in ( ) to complete each sentence.

1. One (woman, women) is working.

2. Many (men, man) are on horses.

3. A (child, children) is wading in the stream.

4. He has no shoes on his (feet, foot).

5. The cold water makes his (teeth, tooth) chatter.

DIRECTIONS Make the noun in ( ) mean more than one. Write the plural noun to complete the sentence.

6. The _____ pet the dogs.
   (child)

7. The little dog has big _____.
   (foot)

8. The big dog has little _____.
   (tooth)

9. Those _____ feed the dogs.
   (man)

10. Those _____ walk the dogs.
    (woman)

Other Irregular Plural Nouns

Nouns that end in <u>f</u> or <u>fe</u> often change spelling to name more than one.

Examples:

calf—calves	hoof—hooves
elf—elves	knife—knives
shelf—shelves	wife—wives
wolf—wolves	

DIRECTIONS **Circle the correct noun in ( ) to complete each sentence.**

1. I keep my books on a tall (shelf, shelves).

2. One book is about a king with seven (wife, wives).

3. Another book tells about a magic (elf, elves).

4. My favorite story is about a boy who lives with (wolf, wolves).

DIRECTIONS **Write a sentence with each irregular plural.**

5. calves _____

_____

6. knives _____

_____

7. hooves _____

_____

Pronouns

A **pronoun** is a word that takes the place of one or more nouns.
Example:

The mouse and the lion are friends.
They are friends.

The pronouns I, we, he, she, it, and they are used in the naming part of a sentence.
Example:

The mouse helped the lion.
She helped the lion.

DIRECTIONS **Read the sentences. Think of a pronoun for the underlined words. Write the pronoun on the line.**

1. The mouse and I live in the woods. _____

2. The mouse fell into the spring. _____

3. The lion saw the mouse fall. _____

4. The leaf landed in the water. _____

5. A hunter spread a net. _____

6. The net was for the lion. _____

7. The mouse and the lion helped each other. _____

8. The mouse and I will always be friends. _____

9. The mouse and the lion are happy. _____

10. The mouse and I will watch out for the hunter. _____

Practice with Pronouns

Remember, a pronoun is a word that takes the place of one or more nouns. The pronouns <u>I</u>, <u>we</u>, <u>he</u>, <u>she</u>, <u>it</u>, and <u>they</u> are used in the naming part of the sentence.

DIRECTIONS ➤ **Finish the story. Use the pronouns from the box.**

We	She	They	He	I	It

My family is very big. _____ live in a house with three bedrooms. My sister Ava is five years old. _____ is the youngest. Ava shares her room with Lily. _____ sing and make music all day in their room. My brothers Todd and Ted are twins. _____ share a room with Bill. _____ says that Todd and Ted snore. _____ am glad that I have my own room! _____ is small but very quiet.

Using I or Me

> The word I is always used in the naming part of a sentence.
> I is always written with a capital letter.
> *Example:*
> > I go to school.
>
> When you speak of or write about another person and yourself, always name yourself last.
> *Example:*
> > Tina and I are in the same class.
>
> The word me follows a verb, or action word.
> *Examples:*
> > Tina makes me laugh.
> > The teacher tells Tina and me to be quiet.

DIRECTIONS → **Write I or me to complete each sentence correctly.**

1. _____ am taking a test.

2. The teacher tells _____ to stop laughing.

3. Mother takes _____ home.

4. _____ have fun with Tina.

DIRECTIONS → **Read the sentences. Circle the correct words in ( ) to complete each sentence.**

5. (Susan and I, I and Susan) are friends.

6. The teacher tells (Tina and me, me and Tina) to hush.

7. (I and Tina, Tina and I) eat lunch together.

8. Mr. Smith asks (Susan and me, Susan and I) to pass out the papers.

Using We or Us

The word <u>we</u> is always used in the naming part of a sentence.
Example:
   <u>We</u> like pizza.
The word <u>us</u> follows a verb, or action word.
Examples:
   Dad made <u>us</u> pizza.
   He let <u>us</u> choose the toppings.

DIRECTIONS Write <u>we</u> or <u>us</u> to complete each sentence correctly. Remember to use a capital letter if the word comes at the beginning of a sentence.

1. _____ are going to the circus.

2. Mom and Dad will take _____ on Saturday.

3. _____ will see clowns.

4. They will make _____ laugh.

5. The animals will show _____ tricks.

6. _____ will have a great time.

DIRECTIONS Read the sentences. Circle the correct words in ( ) to complete each sentence.

7. After the game, Mom drove (we, us) home.

8. (We, Us) were all tired.

9. The other team almost beat (we, us).

10. Then (we, us) made three goals.

11. (We, Us) won the game.

Action Verbs

An **action verb** is a word that shows action. Verbs tell what a person, place, or thing does.

Examples:

People <u>drive</u> across the country.

We <u>walk</u> to school.

DIRECTIONS ➤ **Circle the verb in each sentence.**

1. Eric runs by Mr. and Mrs. Wilson's house.

2. He kicks a football into the air.

3. The ball breaks the Wilsons' window.

4. Mrs. Wilson looks out the door.

5. Mr. Wilson shakes his head.

6. Eric's face turns red.

7. Eric runs inside his house.

8. Mother talks to Eric about the window.

9. Mother sends Eric to the Wilsons' house.

10. Eric pays for the window.

DIRECTIONS ➤ **Draw a line from each noun to the correct action verb.**

Nouns	Verbs
11. The boy	hops.
12. The baby	sing.
13. The rabbit	bark.
14. The birds	cries.
15. The dogs	reads.

Practice with Action Verbs

Remember, an action verb shows action. Verbs tell what a person, place, or thing does.
Examples:
  We <u>play</u> checkers.
  Ethan <u>wins</u> every time!

 Choose an action verb from the box to complete each sentence.

laugh	lives	walk	makes	tells	waves

1. Jacob _____ in the house next door.

2. We _____ to school together.

3. Jacob _____ me stories about his class.

4. He _____ his arms.

5. He _____ funny faces.

6. I _____ at his stories.

DIRECTIONS Write an action verb to complete each sentence.

7. At recess, I _____ hopscotch.

8. When I get tired, I _____ in the shade.

9. Sometimes I _____ with my friends.

10. Sometimes I _____ alone.

Singular Verbs

Add <u>s</u> to an action verb that tells about one person or thing.
Examples:
    The pirate <u>walks</u> quickly.
    He <u>sees</u> his friends.

 DIRECTIONS **Read the sentences. Circle the correct verb in ( ) to complete each sentence.**

1. The cat (skip, skips) down the steps.

2. Two cats (play, plays) on the stairs.

3. The children (hug, hugs) the cat.

4. The cat (purr, purrs) happily.

5. A puppy (bark, barks) at the cat.

6. The boys (hide, hides) from the girls.

7. An ape (wave, waves) to them.

8. The wind (blow, blows) the trees.

9. My shadow (follow, follows) me.

10. A girl (see, sees) a shadow.

11. Mary (hear, hears) the tree speak.

12. The branches (move, moves) in the wind.

13. An owl (hoot, hoots) in the tree.

14. The children (take, takes) their treats home.

15. They (eat, eats) some fruit.

Practice with Singular Verbs

Remember to add <u>s</u> to an action verb that tells about one person or thing.
Examples:

      The boy <u>wants</u> an apple.
      My sister <u>loves</u> her kitten.

DIRECTIONS   **Circle the singular verbs in the story.**

1.   It is a rainy day. We stay inside. Margo reads a book in the den. Dad takes a nap in his room. Mom rests on the couch. The baby sleeps in her crib. The dog snores in its bed. I guess I can't practice the piano right now.

DIRECTIONS   **Circle the correct verb in ( ) to complete each sentence.**

2. Ella (skate, skates) every Saturday at the skating rink.

3. She (wear, wears) pink ice skates.

4. Her coach (teach, teaches) her new moves.

5. The other students (learn, learns), too.

6. They all (practice, practices) together.

7. Sometimes Ella's mom (come, comes) to watch her skate.

8. She always (clap, claps) after Ella (perform, performs).

Helping Verbs

A **helping verb** works with the main verb to show action.
Use <u>has</u>, <u>have</u>, and <u>had</u> with other verbs to show action that happened in the past.
Examples:
Chen <u>has</u> worked hard.
Brit and Katie <u>have</u> helped.
They <u>had</u> stopped earlier for a snack.

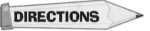 **DIRECTIONS** ➤ **Circle the helping verb in each sentence.**

1. Now we have arrived at the camp.

2. Tom and Bill have unloaded the car.

3. Mr. Green had shopped for food the day before.

4. Bob has gathered firewood.

5. Something strange has happened.

6. A spaceship has landed nearby!

DIRECTIONS ➤ **Circle the correct helping verb in ( ) to complete each sentence.**

7. We (has, have) built a new playground.

8. Mom and Dad (had, has) sawed the boards before.

9. Donna (has, have) sanded the wood.

10. They (has, have) painted the fence.

11. My brother and I (has, have) raked the leaves.

12. But my mother (had, have) forgotten the leaf bags.

Verbs That Do Not Show Action

Some verbs do not show action. They tell about being.
Examples:

A snake <u>is</u> a reptile.

The snake <u>was</u> hungry.

Use <u>am</u> or <u>was</u> with the word <u>I</u>.
Examples:

I <u>am</u> in the tree.

I <u>was</u> under the tree.

Use <u>is</u> or <u>was</u> with one person or thing. Use <u>are</u> or <u>were</u> with more than one person or thing.
Examples:

A lizard <u>is</u> in my garden.

Two turtles <u>were</u> in a box.

DIRECTIONS ⟫ **Read the sentences. Circle the correct verb in ( ) to complete each sentence.**

1. Reptiles (are, is) cold-blooded animals.

2. Some snakes (are, is) dangerous.

3. Many kinds of lizards (were, was) at the zoo.

4. A draco (is, am) a lizard.

5. Crocodiles (are, is) the largest reptiles.

6. The crocodiles (were, was) very noisy.

7. One lizard (is, are) in the box.

8. I (is, am) near the turtle's box.

9. The box (was, were) near the window.

10. The turtle (is, are) sleeping.

Present-Tense Verbs

Present-tense verbs tell about action that happens now.
Example:

Max and Lisa <u>walk</u> to school.

Add <u>s</u> to an action verb that tells about one person or thing.
Example:

Lisa <u>walks</u> to school.

DIRECTIONS Read the sentences. Circle the correct verb in ( ) to complete each sentence.

1. Max (play, plays) baseball.

2. He (run, runs) fast.

3. The girls (dance, dances) to the music.

4. Some friends (wait, waits) for Max.

5. Lisa (leap, leaps) across the floor.

DIRECTIONS Finish the story. Add action verbs. You may use words from the box.

sits	stands	asks	takes	walks	dances

Max _____ his sister to her dancing class.
He _____ on a chair to watch. The teacher
_____ him to join the class. First, he
_____ with a girl. Then, he _____
by a wall. Last, he _____ home.

More Present-Tense Verbs

Remember, present-tense verbs tell about action that happens now.
Example:
> Sam and Olivia <u>eat</u> apples.

Add <u>s</u> to an action verb that tells about one person or thing.
Example:
> Parker <u>eats</u> a pear.

DIRECTIONS ▷ Read the sentences. Circle the correct verb in ( ) to complete each sentence.

1. Maddie (paint, paints) pictures.

2. She (use, uses) many colors.

3. Her parents (hang, hangs) her pictures in the living room.

4. Visitors (look, looks) at the pictures.

5. They (say, says) Maddie is talented.

DIRECTIONS ▷ Finish each sentence using a present-tense verb.

6. My dog _____ in the yard.

7. I _____ her because she is muddy.

8. I _____ her to stay out of the dirt.

9. As soon as I clean her, she _____ outside again!

More Present-Tense Verbs

Past-Tense Verbs

Past-tense verbs can tell about actions in the past. Form the past tense of most verbs by adding <u>ed</u>.

Example:

    Mary Jo <u>planted</u> vegetables yesterday.

DIRECTIONS   Make each sentence tell about the past. Circle the correct verb in ( ) to complete each sentence.

1. Jeff (plays, played) with his sister.

2. The family (visited, visits) Grandmother often.

3. Mary Jo (looks, looked) out the window.

4. Then, she (jumped, jumps) up and down.

5. Grandmother (leans, leaned) back on the pillow.

6. Mary Jo (helps, helped) Grandmother.

7. Grandmother (laughs, laughed) at the baby chicks.

DIRECTIONS   Change each sentence. Make the verb tell about the past. Write the new sentence.

8. The girls play in the park.

    _____

9. They climb over rocks.

    _____

10. Their fathers call to them.

    _____

More Past-Tense Verbs

Remember, verbs can tell about actions in the past. Form the past tense of most verbs by adding ed.

Examples:

The girls talked to their mother.
The horse jumped over the fence.
I laughed at the joke.

 DIRECTIONS Make each sentence tell about the past. Circle the correct verb in ( ) to complete each sentence.

1. Jake (wants, wanted) to make his mom's birthday special.

2. He (baked, bakes) a cake with his dad's help.

3. He (walks, walked) to the store to buy a gift.

4. He (signs, signed) a big card.

5. He (picked, picks) some flowers from the garden.

6. That night, Jake (surprised, surprises) his mom.

7. His mom (looks, looked) very happy.

DIRECTIONS Finish each sentence using a past-tense verb.

8. Last year, I _____ every day at recess.

9. Emily and I _____ on the monkey bars.

10. We _____ with jump ropes.

11. When Mr. Hill _____ us back to class, we were tired.

Irregular Verbs

Some action verbs do not add <u>ed</u> to tell about the past.

Present	Past
go, goes	went
come, comes	came
run, runs	ran

Examples:

The boys <u>went</u> to sleep.

A dog <u>came</u> to a farm.

The raccoons <u>ran</u> into the woods.

DIRECTIONS Read the sentences. Circle the correct verb in ( ) to complete each sentence.

1. Three robbers (ran, runs) out the door.

2. They (comes, came) back.

3. Four animals (goes, went) by the house.

4. The rooster and the dog (go, goes) into the kitchen.

5. The friends (run, runs) down the road.

6. A cat (goes, go) very fast.

DIRECTIONS Circle the verb in each sentence. Then, write each verb in the past tense.

7. The man goes to the mill. _____

8. A donkey comes to town. _____

9. The animals come to a big house. _____

10. They run to the window. _____

More Irregular Verbs

Here are some other action verbs that do not add <u>ed</u> to tell about the past.

Present: bring, do, does, fall, eat, fly, flies, sell, break

Past: brought, did, fell, ate, flew, sold, broke

Example:

He got sick after he <u>ate</u> seven hamburgers.

DIRECTIONS Read the sentences. Circle the correct past-tense verb in ( ) to complete each sentence.

1. We (brought, bring) valentines to school last February.

2. Last week, I (fall, fell) down the stairs.

3. What (did, do) you do at school today?

4. Last summer, we (fly, flew) to Maine on an airplane.

5. My brother (breaks, broke) the dish last night.

6. Yesterday, I (sold, sell) a glass of lemonade to Mr. Green.

7. At the party, I (eat, ate) two slices of cake.

DIRECTIONS Circle the verb in each sentence. Then, write each verb in the past tense.

8. A bird flies through the window. _____

9. It breaks Mom's favorite vase. _____

10. How does it get in here? _____

Adding ed or ing to Verbs

To show that something happened in the past, add <u>ed</u> to most verbs.
Example:
> Don <u>visited</u> Liz yesterday.

To show that something is happening now, you can add <u>ing</u> to most verbs.
Example:
> Sue is <u>visiting</u> Liz now.

DIRECTIONS Circle the correct verb in ( ) to complete each sentence.

1. Terry and Joe (played, playing) basketball last week.

2. Jenna (called, calling) to them.

3. She (wanted, wanting) to play, too.

4. The boys (laughed, laughing) at her.

5. But Jenna (jumped, jumping) for the ball.

6. She (played, playing) well.

7. Terry and Joe are not (laughed, laughing) anymore.

8. Now, Jenna is (played, playing) on their team.

9. Everyone is (talked, talking) about all the games they've won.

DIRECTIONS Add <u>ed</u> or <u>ing</u> to each verb. Then, rewrite each sentence.

10. Carmen help _____ Grandma cook yesterday.

_____

11. Grandma is cook _____ some soup today.

_____

Using Is or Are

Use is and are to tell about something that is happening now.
Use is to tell about one person, place, or thing. Use are to tell about
more than one person, place, or thing. Use are with the word you.
Examples:

     Judy is going.
     Lynne and Ed are skating.
     The cats are sleeping.
     You are lost. Are you scared?

DIRECTIONS   **Write is or are to complete each sentence correctly.**

1. We _____ going to the park.

2. Al _____ going, too.

3. Kate and Mario _____ running.

4. She _____ the faster runner.

5. Where _____ the twins?

6. They _____ climbing a tree.

7. You _____ going to climb, too.

8. The children _____ having fun.

DIRECTIONS   **Write one sentence about a park using is. Then, write one sentence about a park using are.**

9. (is) _____

10. (are) _____

Practice Using <u>Is</u> or <u>Are</u>

Remember, use <u>is</u> and <u>are</u> to tell about something that is happening now. Use <u>is</u> to tell about one person, place, or thing. Use <u>are</u> to tell about more than one person, place, or thing. Use <u>are</u> with the word <u>you</u>.

Examples:

We <u>are</u> taking a walk.

She <u>is</u> swimming.

Arnold <u>is</u> painting the house.

DIRECTIONS Write <u>is</u> or <u>are</u> to complete each sentence correctly.

1. Dad _____ building us a tree house.

2. We _____ helping him.

3. Emma and Anna _____ sanding the wood.

4. They _____ wearing gloves.

5. Mom _____ nailing the wood together.

6. She _____ very busy.

7. Matt and I _____ painting the wood.

8. We _____ excited to see the house when it is finished.

DIRECTIONS Write one sentence about a tree house using <u>is</u>. Then, write one sentence about a tree house using <u>are</u>.

9. (is) _____

10. (are) _____

Using <u>Was</u> or <u>Were</u>

Use <u>was</u> and <u>were</u> to tell about something that happened
in the past. Use <u>was</u> to tell about one person, place, or thing. Use
<u>were</u> to tell about more than one person, place, or thing. Use <u>were</u>
with the word <u>you</u>.

Examples:

My bat <u>was</u> on the step.
Ten people <u>were</u> there.
You <u>were</u> late. <u>Were</u> you home?

DIRECTIONS Circle the correct verb in ( ) to complete each sentence.

1. The children (was, were) indoors while it rained.

2. José (was, were) reading a book.

3. Scott and Jay (was, were) playing checkers.

4. Ann, Roy, and Jami (was, were) playing cards.

5. Sara and Tara (was, were) talking.

6. Nick (was, were) beating a drum.

7. I (was, were) drawing pictures.

8. You (was, were) dancing.

DIRECTIONS Write one sentence about a rainy day using <u>was</u>. Then,
write one sentence about a rainy day using <u>were</u>.

9. (was) _____

10. (were) _____

Practice Using <u>Was</u> or <u>Were</u>

Remember, use <u>was</u> or <u>were</u> to tell about something that happened in the past. Use <u>was</u> to tell about one person, place, or thing. Use <u>were</u> to tell about more than one person, place, or thing.

DIRECTIONS Circle the correct verb in ( ) to complete each sentence in the story.

Dad and Lila (were, was) at the baseball field. Alex and I (were, was) watching a movie. My mom (were, was) watching it with us. We (was, were) eating popcorn. Alex (was, were) a little scared. I (were, was) scared, too. Alex, Mom, and I (were, was) watching the movie very carefully. We didn't hear Dad and Lila come home. They (were, was) standing right behind us. When we saw them, we (was, were) so surprised that we screamed. We spilled popcorn everywhere! Dad and Lila (were, was) laughing at our surprise. Soon, we (was, were) all laughing!

DIRECTIONS Write a sentence to tell what happens next in the story.

_____

_____

Using See, Sees, or Saw

Use <u>see</u> or <u>sees</u> to tell what is happening now. Use <u>see</u> with the words <u>you</u> and <u>I</u>. Use <u>saw</u> to tell what happened in the past.
Examples:
One boy <u>sees</u> a dog. Two boys <u>see</u> a dog.
I <u>see</u> a dog. Do you <u>see</u> a dog?
Justin <u>saw</u> Natalie last week.

DIRECTIONS ➤ **Write <u>see</u>, <u>sees</u>, or <u>saw</u> to complete each sentence correctly.**

1. Today Mike _____ his friend Lori.

2. He _____ her last Monday.

3. Lori _____ Mike paint now.

4. My dad _____ Mike paint now, too.

5. Mike _____ a beautiful sky last night.

6. He _____ pink in the sky on Sunday.

7. Grandpa and I _____ some trains now.

8. We _____ many trains on my last birthday.

9. We _____ old and new trains last winter.

10. Today I can _____ the train show.

DIRECTIONS ➤ **Write <u>see</u>, <u>sees</u>, or <u>saw</u>. Then, rewrite each sentence.**

11. Last week we _____ Lee.

_____

12. Lee _____ my painting now.

_____

Using <u>Run</u>, <u>Runs</u>, or <u>Ran</u>

Use <u>run</u> or <u>runs</u> to tell what is happening now. Use <u>run</u> with the words <u>you</u> and <u>I</u>. Use <u>ran</u> to tell what happened in the past.
Examples:
> One horse <u>runs</u>. Two horses <u>run</u>.
> I <u>run</u> in the park. Do you <u>run</u>?
> Yesterday we <u>ran</u> to the park.

○○○○○○○○○○○○○○○○○○○○○○○○○○○○○○○○○○

DIRECTIONS **Write <u>run</u>, <u>runs</u>, or <u>ran</u>. Then, rewrite each sentence.**

1. Horses _____ wild long ago.

_____

2. A horse can _____ ten miles every day.

_____

3. Can you _____ as fast as a horse?

_____

4. Mandy _____ in a race last week.

_____

5. Carl _____ home from school now.

_____

6. Now Mandy _____ after Carl.

_____

7. How far can you _____?

_____

Using <u>Give</u>, <u>Gives</u>, or <u>Gave</u>

Use <u>give</u> or <u>gives</u> to tell what is happening now. Use <u>give</u> with the words <u>you</u> and <u>I</u>. Use <u>gave</u> to tell what happened in the past.
Examples:
> One student <u>gives</u> a gift. Two students <u>give</u> a gift.
> I <u>give</u> a gift. Do you <u>give</u> one?
> Jenna <u>gave</u> me a present yesterday.

> **DIRECTIONS** **Read the sentences. Circle the correct verb in ( ) to complete each sentence.**

1. Can you (give, gives, gave) the animals some food?

2. Sandi (give, gives, gave) them water yesterday.

3. Juan (give, gives, gave) the chickens corn now.

4. Chickens (give, gives, gave) us eggs to eat yesterday.

5. We (give, gives, gave) the kittens some milk last night.

6. Who (give, gives, gave) hay to the cow then?

7. Our cow (give, gives, gave) us milk yesterday.

8. I (give, gives, gave) food to the pigs last Monday.

> **DIRECTIONS** **Write three sentences about gifts using <u>give</u>, <u>gives</u>, and <u>gave</u>.**

9. (give) _____

10. (gives) _____

11. (gave) _____

Using Do or Does

Use <u>does</u> to tell about one person, place, or thing.
Use <u>do</u> to tell about more than one person, place,
or thing. Also use <u>do</u> with the words <u>you</u> and <u>I</u>.
Examples:

     William <u>does</u> the work.

     They <u>do</u> the work.

     I <u>do</u> the work. You <u>do</u> the work.

DIRECTIONS ▷ Write <u>do</u> or <u>does</u> to complete each sentence correctly.

1. We _____ a lot of work in the house.

2. My dad _____ all the dishes.

3. My mom _____ the windows.

4. My sister _____ the sweeping.

5. My grandma _____ the sewing.

6. I _____ the floor.

7. My little brother _____ the dusting.

8. I _____ not cook dinner.

9. My little sister _____ put away toys.

10. We all _____ some work in our house.

DIRECTIONS ▷ Write one sentence about yourself using <u>do</u>. Then, write one sentence about a friend using <u>does</u>.

11. _____

12. _____

Using <u>Has</u>, <u>Have</u>, or <u>Had</u>

Use <u>has</u> to tell about one person, place, or thing. Use <u>have</u> to tell about more than one person, place, or thing. Use <u>have</u> with the words <u>you</u> and <u>I</u>. Use <u>had</u> to tell about the past.
Examples:

Jesse <u>has</u> a bird.

Cars <u>have</u> tires.

You <u>have</u> new shoes. I <u>have</u> fun.

My dogs <u>had</u> fleas. Bill <u>had</u> a cat last year.

> **DIRECTIONS**   Circle the correct verb in ( ) to complete each sentence.

1. My brother (has, have, had) a pet fish last year.

2. Now Dan (has, have, had) a pet mouse.

3. The pets (has, have, had) good homes now.

4. I (has, have, had) a football now.

5. Now Dana (has, have, had) a pair of roller skates, too.

6. Yesterday Dawn (has, have, had) a full balloon.

7. Now the balloon (has, have, had) a hole in it.

8. She (has, have, had) the money to buy another balloon today.

> **DIRECTIONS**   Write <u>has</u>, <u>have</u>, or <u>had</u> to complete each sentence correctly.

9. You _____ many friends now.

10. Your friends _____ fun together last Saturday.

11. Last week I _____ supper with Eric.

12. Now he _____ supper with me.

Practice Using <u>Has</u>, <u>Have</u>, or <u>Had</u>

Remember, use <u>has</u> to tell about one person, place, or thing.
Use <u>have</u> to tell about more than one person, place, or thing.
Also use <u>have</u> with the words <u>you</u> and <u>I</u>.
Use <u>had</u> to tell about the past.
Examples:
    Maria <u>has</u> a book.
    We <u>have</u> pizza for dinner.
    You <u>have</u> red hair. I <u>have</u> brown hair.
    I <u>had</u> a green crayon.

> **DIRECTIONS** Circle the correct word in ( ) to complete each sentence in the story.

My baby brother, Brady, is seven months old. He (has, had, have) two teeth. He also (has, had, have) a problem. He chews on everything! Last week, my mom (has, had, have) a cookie in her hand. Brady tried to bite it. Yesterday, my sister (has, had, have) a book in her backpack. Brady tried to eat it. This morning, my dad (has, had, have) keys in his hand. Brady tried to munch them. Now I have a big balloon. Maybe I should hide it. Brady will try to swallow it. Sometimes, it is hard to (has, had, have) a baby brother!

Adjectives

An **adjective** is a describing word. A describing word describes a noun.

Example:

The <u>old</u> woman walked home.

Describing words can tell about color or size.

Example:

<u>Red</u> flowers grow in the <u>small</u> garden.

Describing words can tell about shape.

Example:

The house has a <u>square</u> window.

Describing words can tell how something feels, tastes, sounds, or smells.

Example:

The flowers have a <u>sweet</u> smell.

DIRECTIONS Finish the sentences. Add describing words from the box.

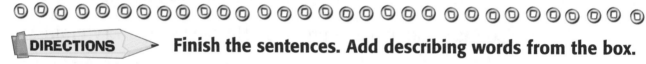

| round | long | brown | tiny | pink | juicy |

1. The woman puts on a _____ bonnet.

2. She walks down a _____ road.

3. Some _____ squirrels run by.

4. A man gives her a _____ orange.

5. The orange is _____.

6. Do you see a _____ bone in the yard?

Practice with Adjectives

Remember, adjectives are describing words.
Describing words can describe feelings.
Examples:

    The woman was <u>surprised</u>.

    She was <u>happy</u>.

Describing words can also tell how many.
Example:

    She picked <u>four</u> flowers.

Some describing words that tell how many do not tell exact numbers.
Examples:

    There are <u>many</u> roses in the garden.

    <u>Some</u> grass grows here.

DIRECTIONS   **Finish the sentences. Add describing words from the box.**

happy	some	hungry	tired	three	sleepy	one	many

1. The woman was _____ from walking so far.

2. She was _____ to be home.

3. First, she put _____ flowers in a vase.

4. Next, she put _____ bone in a pot.

5. She was _____ and wanted to eat.

6. Then, she ate _____ soup.

7. She also had _____ crackers.

8. The woman was _____ and went to bed.

Adjectives That Compare

Add <u>er</u> to most describing words when they are used to compare two things.
Example:
This tree is <u>taller</u> than that one.
Add <u>est</u> to most describing words when they are used to compare more than two things.
Example:
The sequoia tree is the <u>tallest</u> tree of all.

DIRECTIONS Read the chart. Fill in the missing describing words.

1.	long	longer	longest
2.	bright		brightest
3.	tall	taller	
4.		faster	fastest

DIRECTIONS Circle the correct describing word in ( ) to complete each sentence.

5. That tree trunk is (thick, thicker) than this one.

6. The giant sequoia is the (bigger, biggest) living plant of all.

7. The stump of a giant sequoia is (wider, widest) than my room.

8. These trees are the (older, oldest) of all.

More Adjectives That Compare

Usually, <u>er</u> is added to a describing word when it is used to compare two things. When more than two things are being compared, <u>est</u> is usually added to the describing word.

However, not all words follow this rule. <u>Good</u> is one word that changes spelling when it is used to compare things. <u>Good</u> becomes <u>better</u> when it is used to compare two things. It become <u>best</u> when used to compare more than two things.

Examples:

That diner makes <u>good</u> hamburgers.

I think that they have <u>better</u> burgers at Sam's Place.

My dad makes the <u>best</u> burgers in the world.

<u>Bad</u> is another word that changes spelling when it is used to compare things. <u>Bad</u> becomes <u>worse</u> when it is used to compare two things. It becomes <u>worst</u> when used to compare more than two things.

Examples:

Monday was <u>bad</u>.

Tuesday was <u>worse</u> than Monday.

Today is the <u>worst</u> day ever!

DIRECTIONS ▷ **Circle the correct word in ( ) to complete each sentence.**

1. I liked the first movie, but the second movie was much (good, better, best).

2. An F is the (bad, worse, worst) grade you can get.

3. Mia is the (good, better, best) soccer player at our school.

4. Dad said the traffic is (bad, worse, worst) today than it was yesterday.

5. She is a good dancer, but if she practices, she can become even (good, better, best).

6. This is the (good, better, best) book I have ever read!

Using A or An

A and an are called **articles**. They are special adjectives.
Use an before words that begin with a vowel sound. The vowels
are a, e, i, o, and u.
Use a before words that begin with a consonant sound.
Examples:

> an apple, an egg
> a car, a skate

DIRECTIONS Choose the correct article. Write a or an before each word.

1. _____ arm

2. _____ dog

3. _____ hat

4. _____ ant

5. _____ cat

6. _____ elf

7. _____ ear

8. _____ office

9. _____ fire

10. _____ cow

11. _____ uncle

12. _____ tree

13. _____ inch

14. _____ ax

15. _____ top

16. _____ boat

17. _____ duck

18. _____ eagle

DIRECTIONS Write a or an to complete each sentence correctly.

19. Randy put _____ apple in my box.

20. Victor has _____ old bike.

21. Linda has two balls and _____ bat.

22. I have _____ sweet apple.

Practice Using <u>A</u> or <u>An</u>

Remember to use <u>an</u> before words that begin with a vowel sound.
The vowels are <u>a</u>, <u>e</u>, <u>i</u>, <u>o</u>, and <u>u</u>.
Use <u>a</u> before words that begin with a consonant sound.

DIRECTIONS Fill out the graph below using the animal names from the box. Write each name under the correct adjective.

dog	ape	butterfly	lizard	turtle	snake
owl	eel	bear	iguana	otter	ant

a	an

Sentences

A **sentence** is a group of words that tells or asks something. It gives a complete thought. Every sentence begins with a capital letter. Every sentence ends with a punctuation mark.
Examples:
    Friends play.
    Cars go fast.

> **DIRECTIONS** **Write <u>yes</u> if the group of words is a sentence. Write <u>no</u> if the group of words is not a sentence.**

_____ **1.** A long time ago.

_____ **2.** The class went to the park.

_____ **3.** Near the tree.

_____ **4.** Ten children played.

_____ **5.** Mark hit the ball.

_____ **6.** A dog chased the ball.

_____ **7.** Bill and Tom.

_____ **8.** Ran and played all day.

_____ **9.** Everyone had fun.

_____ **10.** Jan lost a new red shoe.

_____ **11.** We ate lunch.

_____ **12.** Too hot for us.

_____ **13.** The boys and girls talked.

_____ **14.** Some people.

_____ **15.** Then, we went home.

Practice with Sentences

Remember, a sentence tells a complete thought.
Examples:
> Mari caught the ball.
> Chad read a book.

DIRECTIONS ▷ Draw lines between the groups of words to make sentences. Then, read the sentences.

1.	Mrs. Brown	live in our building.
2.	Our building	is made of wood.
3.	Four families	lives on my street.
4.	Our class	was climbing the tree.
5.	Jennifer	went on a picnic.
6.	The sun	shone all day.
7.	Corn and beans	fed the baby goat.
8.	The wagon	has a broken wheel.
9.	The mother goat	grow on a farm.
10.	The boat	sailed in strong winds.
11.	The fisherman	were sold in the store.
12.	Some of the fish	caught seven fish.
13.	Our team	hit the ball a lot.
14.	Our batters	won ten games.
15.	The ballpark	was full of fans.

DIRECTIONS ▷ Write a sentence about your birthday.

16. _____

_____

Sentence Parts

Every sentence has two parts. The **naming part** tells who or what the sentence is about. The naming part is called the subject.
The **action part** tells something about the naming part. The action part is called the predicate.
A naming part and an action part make a complete thought.
Example:

Naming Part	Action Part
Sara	plants some seeds.

DIRECTIONS ▷ Each group of words needs a naming part or an action part. Add words to make each group of words a complete sentence.

1. John _____.

2. Sara _____.

3. _____ need sunshine and rain.

4. The flower seeds _____.

5. John and Sara _____.

6. _____ looks at the flower.

7. _____ grow in the garden.

8. The flowers _____.

9. _____ bloom in the spring.

10. _____ are my favorite flowers.

11. The butterflies _____.

12. _____ makes the flowers grow.

Naming Part of Sentences

Remember, the naming part of a sentence tells who or what the sentence is about.

Examples:

Three mice run away.

The cat plays with a ball.

DIRECTIONS ➤ **Circle the naming part of each sentence.**

1. My family and I live on a busy street.

2. Sami Harper found a bird.

3. Miss Jenkins drives very slowly.

4. Mr. Chang walks his dog.

5. Henry throws a ball.

6. Mr. Byrne cuts his grass.

7. Mrs. Lee picks up her children.

8. Mr. and Mrs. Diaz shop for food.

9. Jeanine plays in the park.

10. Mr. Wolf brings the mail.

11. Amy Taft brings the paper.

12. Mr. Dowd cooks dinner.

13. Mrs. Clark washes her windows.

14. Carolyn and Alberto plant flower seeds.

15. Julie waters the garden.

Action Part of Sentences

Remember, the action part of a sentence tells what someone or something does.
Examples:

    Three mice <u>run away</u>.

    The cat <u>plays with a ball</u>.

DIRECTIONS ▸ **Choose an action part from the box to complete each sentence. Write it on the line.**

barks	buzz	fly	hops	moo	cluck	quack	roar

1. Robins and blackbirds _____.

2. Yellow bees _____.

3. My little dog _____.

4. Mother Duck and her babies _____.

5. A rabbit with big feet _____.

6. Angry lions _____.

7. All the cows on the farm _____.

8. Chickens _____.

DIRECTIONS ▸ **Write a sentence about an animal that you like. Circle the naming part. Underline the action part.**

9. _____

_____

Word Order in Sentences

Words in a sentence must be in an order that makes sense.
Examples:
> Grandpa plays baseball.
> My sister writes stories.

Write each group of words in an order that makes sense. Be sure to put a period at the end of each sentence.

1. brother My apples eats

_____

2. drinks Elizabeth milk

_____

3. butter peanut Kim likes

_____

4. Justin bread wants

_____

5. corn plants Chris

_____

6. a fish Chang caught

_____

7. breakfast cooks Dad

_____

8. his shares Shawn lunch

_____

9. the Rosa grew carrot

_____

Telling Sentences and Asking Sentences

A **telling sentence** is a group of words that tells something. A telling sentence is also called a statement.

Examples:

I fed my pony.

Ponies like to run and play.

An **asking sentence** is a group of words that asks a question. You can answer an asking sentence. An asking sentence is also called a question.

Examples:

How old are you?

Where do you live?

DIRECTIONS ▷ Write <u>telling</u> on the line before the group of words if it is a telling sentence. Write <u>asking</u> on the line before the group of words if it is an asking sentence. Leave the line blank if the group of words is not a sentence.

_____ **1.** Josh loves his pony.

_____ **2.** His name is Zip.

_____ **3.** Do you like horses?

_____ **4.** Fast horses.

_____ **5.** Zip can run fast.

_____ **6.** Over the hill.

_____ **7.** He eats apples.

_____ **8.** Do you eat apples?

_____ **9.** Zip has soft hair.

Kinds of Sentences

A **statement** is a sentence that tells something. It begins with a capital letter. It ends with a period **(.)**.

Example:

John gives some seeds to Sara.

A **question** is a sentence that asks something. It begins with a capital letter. It ends with a question mark **(?)**.

Example:

Will Sara plant seeds?

An **exclamation** is a sentence that shows strong feeling. It begins with a capital letter. It ends with an exclamation point **(!)**.

Example:

What a fine garden John has!

DIRECTIONS Read the sentences. Write <u>statement</u> for a telling sentence. Write <u>question</u> for an asking sentence. Write <u>exclamation</u> for a sentence that shows strong feeling.

_____ **1.** John was in his garden.

_____ **2.** Who came walking by?

_____ **3.** Sara stopped to look at the garden.

_____ **4.** What did Sara do?

_____ **5.** Sara read a story to her seeds.

_____ **6.** Did Sara do anything else?

_____ **7.** Poor Sara fell asleep in her garden!

_____ **8.** The seeds started to grow.

_____ **9.** What makes seeds grow?

_____ **10.** Sara works so hard!

Practice with Kinds of Sentences

Remember, a statement tells something. End a statement with a period (.).

A question asks something. End a question with a question mark (?).

An exclamation shows strong feeling. End an exclamation with an exclamation point (!).

DIRECTIONS ▸ Finish each sentence to make a statement. Be sure to use the correct end mark.

1. My favorite animal is _____

2. My favorite food is _____

3. My favorite color is _____

DIRECTIONS ▸ Finish each sentence to make a question. Be sure to use the correct end mark.

4. What is _____

5. Where _____

6. Why _____

DIRECTIONS ▸ Finish each sentence to make an exclamation. Be sure to use the correct end mark.

7. I love _____

8. It's so _____

Joining Sentences

A good writer can join two short sentences. This makes the sentences more interesting to read. The word <u>and</u> is used to join the sentences.

Sometimes the naming parts of two sentences are the same. The action parts can be joined.

Example:

John planted seeds. John worked in his garden.
John planted seeds <u>and</u> worked in his garden.

How to Join Sentences

1. Look for sentences that have the same naming part.
2. Write the naming part.
3. Look for different action parts. Use the word <u>and</u> to join them.
4. Write the new sentence.

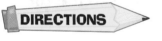 **DIRECTIONS** **Use the word <u>and</u> to join each pair of sentences. Write the new sentences.**

1. John gave seeds to Sara. John told her to plant them.

_____

2. Sara planted the seeds. Sara looked at the ground.

_____

3. Sara sang songs to her seeds. Sara read stories to them.

_____

4. The rain fell on the seeds. The rain helped them grow.

_____

Practice with Joining Sentences

Remember, a good writer can join two short sentences. This makes the sentences more interesting to read. The word <u>and</u> is used to join the sentences.

Sometimes the action parts of two sentences are the same. Then, the naming parts can be joined.

Example:

> The hunter stopped at the house. The bear stopped at the house.
> The hunter <u>and</u> the bear stopped at the house.

How to Join Sentences

1. Look for sentences that have the same action part.
2. Join the naming parts. Use the word <u>and</u>.
3. Add the action part.

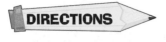 **DIRECTIONS**   **Use the word <u>and</u> to join each pair of sentences. Write the new sentences.**

1. The farmer stood in the doorway. His family stood in the doorway.

_____

2. The hunter stayed with the family. The bear stayed with the family.

_____

3. The mice ran out the door. The children ran out the door.

_____

4. The hunter went home. The bear went home.

_____

Adding Describing Words to Sentences

A good writer adds describing words to sentences to give a clear picture.

Example:

The moth sat on top of a clover.

The <u>black</u> moth sat on top of a <u>green</u> clover.

How to Add Describing Words to Sentences

1. Look for sentences that do not give your reader a clear picture.
2. Think of describing words that tell more about what things look like.
3. Add the describing words to the sentences.

 DIRECTIONS ▷ **Add describing words to these sentences. Write the new sentences.**

1. The clown wears a hat.

_____

2. A lion jumps through a hoop.

_____

3. A monkey rides on an elephant.

_____

4. A butterfly flew into the tent.

_____

Practice with Describing Words

Remember, a good writer adds describing words to sentences to give a clear picture.

Example:

He wore a jacket to school.

He wore a <u>red</u> jacket to school.

You can add one or more describing words to a sentence to make it more interesting.

How to Add Describing Words to Sentences

1. Look for sentences that do not give your reader a clear picture.
2. Think of describing words that tell more about what things look like.
3. Add the describing words to the sentences.

DIRECTIONS ▶ **Add describing words in the blanks to make the story more interesting.**

Anna was excited about the _____ party. She chose a _____ gift. She wrapped it in _____ paper. She put on a _____ dress and _____ shoes. She put a _____ bow in her hair. She walked to Jenny's house. There were lots of _____ balloons tied to the mailbox. Inside, there were many _____ children. There was a _____ cake and _____ presents. The children played _____ games. Anna won a _____ prize. After the party, she told her _____ friend about the _____ day.

Beginning Sentences in Different Ways

A good writer should not begin every sentence with the same noun. Sometimes the words <u>he</u>, <u>she</u>, <u>I</u>, <u>we</u>, and <u>they</u> are used in place of nouns.

Example:

Ant climbed down a branch. Ant was thirsty. <u>She</u> tried to get a drink.

How to Begin Sentences in Different Ways

1. Look for sentences that begin with the same noun.
2. Use the word <u>he</u>, <u>she</u>, <u>I</u>, <u>we</u>, or <u>they</u> in place of the noun.
3. Write the new sentence.

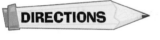 **Change the way some of these sentences begin. Begin some of them with <u>He</u>, <u>She</u>, <u>I</u>, <u>We</u>, or <u>They</u>. Write the new sentences.**

1. The ant climbed down a blade of grass. The ant fell into the spring.

_____

2. The bird pulled off a leaf. The bird let the leaf fall into the water.

_____

3. The hunter saw a lion. The hunter spread his net.

_____

4. The lion and I live in the woods. The lion and I are friends.

_____

Practice with Beginning Sentences

Remember, you can use the words <u>he</u>, <u>she</u>, <u>I</u>, <u>we</u>, and <u>they</u> in place of nouns. This will help make your sentences and stories more interesting.

DIRECTIONS **Read each set of sentences. Rewrite the second sentence so that it begins in a different way. Use <u>He</u>, <u>She</u>, <u>We</u>, or <u>They</u>.**

1. Clare and I were partners for the science fair. Clare and I were doing a project on volcanoes.

_____

2. Robert and Adam were partners, too. Robert and Adam were doing a project on bees.

_____

3. Mrs. Baldwin said that she was proud of how hard everyone was working on the science projects. Mrs. Baldwin is a nice teacher.

_____

4. Clare, Robert, Adam, and I were so excited on the day of the fair. Clare, Robert, Adam, and I all wanted to win.

_____

5. The judges took a lot of time looking at our projects. The judges were writing notes.

_____

6. Mrs. Baldwin made a speech. Mrs. Baldwin told everyone that Robert and Adam had won first prize.

_____

Writing Clear Sentences

A good writer uses exact verbs. These are verbs that give a clear picture of an action.

Example:

Spaceships <u>go</u> to the Moon.
Spaceships <u>zoom</u> to the Moon.

How to Use Exact Verbs in Sentences

1. Picture the action. Think about what a person or thing is doing.
2. Choose an action verb that tells exactly what the person or thing is doing.
3. Use the action verb in a sentence.

 DIRECTIONS   **Think of a more exact verb for each underlined verb. Write the new word on the line.**

1. People <u>walk</u> to work. _____

2. Trains <u>move</u> along the tracks. _____

3. We <u>ride</u> our bicycles. _____

4. Fast cars <u>go</u> up the road. _____

5. The airplane <u>flies</u> in the sky. _____

6. A man <u>runs</u> around the park. _____

7. The children <u>walk</u> to school. _____

8. A bus <u>goes</u> down the highway. _____

9. The boat <u>moves</u> along the shore. _____

Writing Names of People

> Each word of a person's name begins with a capital letter.
> *Examples:*
> Mary Ann Miller
> Michael Jordan
> Grandma Moses

DIRECTIONS Rewrite the names. Use capital letters where they are needed.

1. mark twain _____

2. beverly cleary _____

3. diane dillon _____

4. alicia acker _____

5. ezra jack keats _____

DIRECTIONS Circle the letters that should be capital letters.

6. Today mother called grandma.

7. We will see grandma and grandpa at the party.

8. Will uncle carlos and aunt kathy be there, too?

DIRECTIONS Rewrite the sentences. Use capital letters where they are needed.

9. mario martinez told me a story.

_____

10. ichiro and I played ball.

_____

Writing Initials

An **initial** stands for a person's name. It is a capital letter with a period **(.)** after it.

Examples:

Steven Bell Mathis = Steven **B**. Mathis or **S. B.** Mathis or **S. B. M.**

DIRECTIONS Write the initials of each name.

1. Clara Delrio _____

2. Carrie Anne Collier _____

3. Marcus Brown _____

4. Michael Tond _____

5. Keiko Senda _____

6. Terri Lynn Turner _____

7. Isaiah Bradley _____

8. Cata Lil Walker _____

DIRECTIONS Rewrite the names. Use initials for the names that are underlined.

9. <u>Joan</u> <u>Walsh</u> <u>Anglund</u>

_____

10. <u>Lee</u> <u>Bennett</u> Hopkins

_____

11. <u>Arturo</u> Martinez

_____

12. Patricia <u>Ann</u> Rosen

_____

DIRECTIONS Rewrite the sentences. Be sure to write the initials correctly.

13. The box was for m s mills.

_____

14. d e ellis sent it to her.

_____

15. t j lee brought the box to the house.

_____

69

Writing Titles of Respect

Begin a title of respect with a capital letter.
End <u>Mr.</u>, <u>Mrs.</u>, <u>Ms.</u>, and <u>Dr.</u> with a period. They are short forms, or abbreviations, of longer words.
Do not end <u>Miss</u> with a period.
Examples:
   Mr. George Selden
   Dr. Martin Luther King
   Miss Jane Pittman

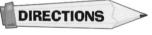
DIRECTIONS ⟶ **Rewrite the names correctly. Place periods and capital letters where they are needed.**

1. mrs ruth scott _____

2. mr kurt wiese _____

3. miss e garcia _____

4. dr seuss _____

5. ms carol baylor _____

6. mr and mrs h cox _____

7. miss k e jones _____

8. dr s tomas rios _____

DIRECTIONS ⟶ **Rewrite the sentences correctly. Place periods and capital letters where they are needed.**

9. mrs h stone is here to see dr brooks.

_____

10. mr f green and ms miller are not here.

_____

Writing Names of Places

The names of cities, states, and countries begin with a capital letter.
The names of streets, parks, lakes, rivers, and schools begin with a capital letter.
The abbreviations of the words <u>street</u>, <u>road</u>, and <u>drive</u> in a place name begin with a capital letter and end with a period.

Examples:

Reno, Nevada
Canada
First Street
Central Park
Red River
Road = Rd.   Dove Rd.

DIRECTIONS ⟩ **Rewrite the sentences. Use capital letters where they are needed.**

1. James lives in dayton, ohio.

_____

2. His house is on market st.

_____

3. I think thomas park is in this town.

_____

4. We went to mathis lake for a picnic.

_____

5. Is perry school far away?

_____

Practice with Place Names

Remember, the names of cities, states, and countries begin with a capital letter. The names of streets, parks, lakes, rivers, and schools begin with a capital letter. The abbreviations of the words <u>street</u>, <u>road</u>, and <u>drive</u> in a place name begin with a capital letter and end with a period.

DIRECTIONS ▷ **Answer each question with a sentence that includes a place name. Remember to use capital letters for all place names.**

1. What is the name of your state? _____

2. What is the name of your city or town? _____

3. What is the name of the street where you live?

_____

4. What is the name of your school? _____

5. What is the name of a park, river, or lake near your house?

_____

6. What is the name of a city or town you have visited?

_____

Practice with Place Names

Writing Names of Days and Months

The names of days of the week begin with a capital letter.
The names of the months begin with a capital letter.
Examples:

Monday, Friday   April, October

The abbreviations of the days of the week begin with a capital letter. They end with a period.
The abbreviations of the months begin with a capital letter. They end with a period. The names of May, June, and July are not usually abbreviated.
Examples:

Sun., Mon., Tues., Wed., Thurs., Fri., Sat.

Jan., Feb., Mar., Apr., Aug., Sept., Oct., Nov., Dec.

DIRECTIONS Write the name of a day or month to complete each sentence.

1. The day after Sunday is _____.

2. The day before Saturday is _____.

3. Valentine's Day is in _____.

4. A month in the summer is _____.

5. Thanksgiving Day is in _____.

DIRECTIONS Write the correct abbreviation for each day or month. Be sure to end the abbreviation with a period.

6. Tuesday _____   **9.** Saturday _____

7. Thursday _____   **10.** January _____

8. December _____   **11.** September _____

Writing Names of Holidays

Each important word in the name of a holiday begins with a capital letter.
Examples:
   Valentine's Day
   Memorial Day
   Fourth of July

DIRECTIONS **Write the holiday names correctly.**

1. new year's day _____

2. mother's day _____

3. independence day _____

4. labor day _____

5. cinco de mayo _____

6. thanksgiving day _____

7. veterans day _____

DIRECTIONS **Rewrite each sentence correctly.**

8. earth day is in April.

_____

9. boxing day is a British holiday.

_____

10. father's day is in June.

_____

Writing Titles of Books, Stories, and Poems

Begin the first word and last word in the title of a book with a capital letter. All other words begin with a capital letter except unimportant words. Some unimportant words are <u>a</u>, <u>an</u>, <u>the</u>, <u>of</u>, <u>with</u>, <u>for</u>, <u>at</u>, <u>in</u>, and <u>on</u>. Draw a line under the title of a book.

Examples:

<u>The Snowy Day</u>

<u>Storm at Sea</u>

Begin the first word, last word, and all important words in the title of a story or poem with a capital letter. Put quotation marks (" ") around the title of a story or poem.

Examples:

"Jonas and the Monster" (story)

"Something Is Out There" (poem)

DIRECTIONS Write these book titles correctly. Be sure to underline the title of a book.

1. best friends

_____

2. the biggest bear

_____

3. rabbits on roller skates

_____

4. down on the sunny farm

_____

 DIRECTIONS Read the sentences. Circle the letters that should be capital letters.

5. My favorite poem is called "we bees."

6. I read a story called "the dancing pony" last week.

7. Robert Louis Stevenson wrote a poem called "my shadow."

8. Lori wrote a story named "my summer on the farm."

Practice with Titles

Remember to use a capital letter for all of the words in a book title except for unimportant words like <u>a</u>, <u>an</u>, <u>of</u>, <u>the</u>, <u>with</u>, <u>for</u>, <u>at</u>, <u>in</u>, and <u>on</u>. Draw a line under the title of a book.
Example:
    <u>The Wind in the Willows</u>
Also, capitalize all the important words in the title of a story or poem. Put quotation marks (**" "**) around the title of a story or poem.
Example:
    "The Cat is Fat"

DIRECTIONS Rewrite each sentence correctly.

1. My mom's favorite book is called gone with the wind.

_____

2. Alison wrote a poem named hay is for horses.

_____

3. At the library, I checked out a book called learn to draw.

_____

4. I read a story about boats called sail away.

_____

5. Mrs. Gibbs read us a poem named a plan for stan.

_____

6. Sara wrote a story called what I did on vacation.

_____

7. Her favorite book is called ramona the great.

_____

Beginning Sentences

Begin the first word of a sentence with a capital letter.
Examples:
>The garden is very pretty.
>Flowers grow there.
>What kind of flowers do you see?

DIRECTIONS > **Rewrite these sentences. Begin each sentence with a capital letter.**

1. there are many kinds of gardens.

_____

2. vegetables grow in some gardens.

_____

3. you can find gardens in parks.

_____

4. i like to work in the garden.

_____

5. deb likes to play ball.

_____

6. her ball is red.

_____

7. jet wants to play.

_____

8. deb throws the ball.

_____

9. the ball goes far.

_____

Ending Sentences

Put a period **(.)** at the end of a sentence that tells something.
Examples:
>Patty is my friend.
>We play together.

Put a question mark **(?)** at the end of a sentence that asks something.
Examples:
>Is he your brother?
>Do you have a sister?

DIRECTIONS ➤ **Rewrite these telling sentences. Use capital letters and periods where they are needed.**

1. patty played on the baseball team

_____

2. patty hit two home runs

_____

3. she caught the ball, too

_____

DIRECTIONS ➤ **Rewrite these asking sentences. Use capital letters and question marks where they are needed.**

4. what time is it

_____

5. is it time for lunch

_____

6. are you ready to eat

_____

Periods

Use a **period (.)** at the end of a statement.
Example:
> I like to read books about frogs.

Put a period at the end of most titles of people.
Example:
> Mr. Arnold Lobel wrote the book.

These are titles of people.
> Mr.   Mrs.   Ms.   Dr.   Miss

DIRECTIONS ➤ **Correct the sentences. Add periods where they are needed.**

1. John has a nice garden

2. The flowers are pretty

3. John gave Sara some seeds

4. Sara will plant them in the ground

5. Little green plants will grow

6. Ms Sara thought the seeds were afraid.

7. Mr John told Sara not to worry.

8. Mrs Jones told Sara to wait a few days.

9. Sara showed her garden to Dr Dewey.

10. Ms Babbitt thinks Sara has a nice garden.

Question Marks, Exclamation Points, and Apostrophes

Use a **question mark (?)** at the end of a question.
Example:
   Who are you?
Use an **exclamation point (!)** at the end of an exclamation.
Example:
   Leave me alone!
Use an **apostrophe (')** to show that one or more letters have been left out in a contraction.
Example:
   His parents didn't take Stewart anywhere.

DIRECTIONS > Finish the sentences correctly. Add question marks and exclamation points where they are needed.

1. Stewart just does not care

2. Does Stewart care about anything

3. Does Stewart care about his grades

4. Yes, indeed he cares

DIRECTIONS > Circle the correct contraction in ( ) to complete each sentence.

5. Stewart said, "I (dont, don't) know what to do!"

6. "(Ill, I'll) help you," said the teacher.

7. Stewart (didn't, didnt) want to get bad grades.

Practice with Question Marks, Exclamation Points, and Apostrophes

Remember, use a question mark (**?**) at the end of a question.
Use an exclamation point (**!**) at the end of an exclamation.
Use an apostrophe (**'**) to show that one or more letters have been left out of a contraction.

DIRECTIONS ▷ **Finish the sentences correctly. Add question marks and exclamation points where they are needed.**

1. Have you ever been camping

2. Do you like to sleep under the stars

3. It is so beautiful

4. Would you like to try it

DIRECTIONS ▷ **Rewrite each sentence using an apostrophe in the contraction.**

5. One thing I dont like is setting up the tent.

_____

6. I cant seem to get it right!

_____

7. Ill ask my mom for help next time.

_____

Using Apostrophes in Contractions

A **contraction** is a word made by joining two words. An **apostrophe**
(') shows where a letter or letters are left out.
Examples:

is not = isn't

cannot = can't

do not = don't

are not = aren't

DIRECTIONS Draw a line from the two words to the contraction.

1. were not   hasn't

2. was not   haven't

3. has not   wasn't

4. have not   weren't

5. did not   aren't

6. are not   didn't

DIRECTIONS Write each contraction as two words.

7. isn't _____ _____

8. don't _____ _____

9. wasn't _____ _____

10. can't _____ _____

11. didn't _____ _____

12. hadn't _____ _____

13. doesn't _____ _____

14. aren't _____ _____

DIRECTIONS Write a contraction for the two words.

15. Today (is not) _____ a good day.

16. I (do not) _____ have my lunch.

17. I (did not) _____ finish my work.

Practice with Contractions

Remember, a contraction is a word made by joining two words. An apostrophe shows where a letter or letters are left out.

Examples:

    does not = doesn't
    were not = weren't
    did not = didn't
    had not = hadn't

DIRECTIONS ▶ **Write a contraction for the two words.**

1. Please (do not) _____ come into my room.

2. I (can not) _____ play because I have to do my homework.

3. I (have not) _____ finished it yet.

4. Mom (does not) _____ like it when I do my homework so late.

5. She says it (is not) _____ a good habit.

DIRECTIONS ▶ **Write a sentence for each contraction.**

6. can't

_____

7. don't

_____

8. weren't

_____

Commas

Use a **comma (,)** between the name of a city and a state.
Examples:
    Toledo, Ohio
    Albany, New York
Use a comma between the day and the year in a date.
Examples:
    July 4, 1776
    November 1, 2003
Use a comma after the greeting and after the closing in a letter.
Examples:
    Dear Mom and Dad,
    Your friend,

DIRECTIONS — **Read Mary Jane's letter to Grandmother. Put commas where they are needed.**

June 8 2005

Dear Grandmother

    I hope you are feeling better. Yesterday Mom and I went shopping. We found a pretty new jacket for you. The tag says it comes from Chicago Illinois. I hope you like the jacket. Please write to me soon.

Love

Mary Jane

Using Commas in Place Names

Put a comma between the name of a city and its state. Names of cities and states begin with a capital letter.

Examples:

    Denver, Colorado
    Dover, Delaware

DIRECTIONS Write the names of the cities and states correctly. Put commas where they are needed.

1. akron ohio   _____

2. hilo hawaii   _____

3. macon georgia   _____

4. nome alaska   _____

5. provo utah   _____

DIRECTIONS Rewrite the sentences. Use capital letters and commas where they are needed.

6. Nancy lives in barnet vermont.

_____

7. Mr. Hill went to houston texas.

_____

8. Did Bruce like bend oregon?

_____

9. Will Amy visit newark ohio?

_____

10. How far away is salem massachusetts?

_____

Using Commas in Dates

Put a comma between the day of the month and the year.
Examples:
March 2, 1836
January 1, 2003

DIRECTIONS Write these dates correctly. Use capital letters, periods, and commas where they are needed.

1. dec 12 1948 _____

2. mar 27 1965 _____

3. sept 8 1994 _____

4. nov 1 2000 _____

5. jan 5 1995 _____

DIRECTIONS Complete the sentences. Write the date correctly on the line.

6. Jim was born on _____. (august 10 1967)

7. Jen's birthday is _____. (Oct 17 1983)

8. Maria visited on _____. (february 8 1991)

9. Dad's party was on _____. (july 29 1989)

10. Carrie started school on _____. (sept 3 2001)

11. Luis lost his first tooth on _____. (oct 20 1998)

12. I was born on _____.

Rhyming Words

Words that end with the same sounds are **rhyming words**. Here are some rhyming words.

Examples:

car—star   boat—goat

A **rhyme** is two or more lines that end with rhyming words. Many rhymes are silly or funny.

Example:

The cat took a rocket trip to the <u>moon</u>.

It left in July and came back in <u>June</u>.

How to Write a Rhyme
1. Write two lines.
2. End each line with a rhyming word.

DIRECTIONS ▷ **Choose a word from the box to finish each rhyme.**

cow	dog	bee	hat

1. Did you ever see a cat

Wear a funny _____?

2. The cat climbed up a tree

And sang a song with a _____.

3. The bee said, "Meow,"

And flew away to visit the _____.

4. The cow watched a frog

Hop over a _____.

More Rhyming Words

Remember, words that end with the same sounds are rhyming words.

Examples:

    bat—cat

    bug—rug

A rhyme is two or more lines that end with rhyming words.

Example:

    I think that there's a tiny bug

    Sleeping on my bedroom rug!

DIRECTIONS ➤ **Draw a line between rhyming words.**

1. dog   hat

2. tall   hog

3. mouse   house

4. flat   ball

5. blue   clue

DIRECTIONS ➤ **Now use one of the rhyme pairs you made above to write a rhyme.**

6. _____

_____

_____

_____

Synonyms

Words that mean almost the same thing are called **synonyms**.

Examples:

<u>Grin</u> is a synonym of <u>smile</u>.

<u>Sleep</u> is a synonym of <u>rest</u>.

DIRECTIONS Read each sentence. Find a synonym in the box for each underlined word. Write it on the line.

dog	dad	gift	large	great	home
road	sad	sick	sleep	small	yell

1. I walked across the <u>street</u>. _____

2. I went into my <u>house</u>. _____

3. I was so <u>unhappy</u>. _____

4. I almost felt <u>ill</u>. _____

5. It was my birthday. No one gave me a <u>present</u>. _____

6. Then I saw something <u>little</u>. _____

7. It had <u>big</u> eyes. _____

8. It was a little <u>puppy</u>. _____

9. I began to <u>shout</u>. _____

10. "What a <u>wonderful</u> present!" _____

11. My <u>father</u> did remember my birthday. _____

12. I don't think I will <u>rest</u> tonight. _____

Antonyms

Words that mean the opposite are called **antonyms**.
Examples:

> <u>Up</u> is an antonym of <u>down</u>.
> <u>Day</u> is an antonym of <u>night</u>.

DIRECTIONS ▷ **Draw a line to the antonym for each underlined word.**

1. a <u>hard</u> bed   dark

2. a <u>short</u> story   happy

3. a <u>light</u> color   long

4. <u>off</u> the table   low

5. a <u>sad</u> movie   on

6. a <u>high</u> bridge   soft

DIRECTIONS ▷ **Write the antonym for the underlined word.**

7. When you are not <u>wet</u>, you are _____.
(happy, dry)

8. I like to run <u>fast</u>, not _____.
(slow, far)

9. When food isn't <u>good</u>, it tastes _____.
(hot, bad)

10. Summer is <u>hot</u>, and winter is _____.
(cold, snow)

11. A traffic light turns red for <u>stop</u> and green for _____.
(high, go)

12. Some questions are <u>easy</u>. Others are _____.
(not, hard)

More Synonyms and Antonyms

Remember, words that mean almost the same thing are called synonyms.
Example:

Happy is a synonym of glad.
Words that mean the opposite are called antonyms.
Example:

Huge is an antonym of tiny.

◎◎◎◎◎◎◎◎◎◎◎◎◎◎◎◎◎◎◎◎◎◎◎◎◎◎◎◎◎◎◎◎◎

DIRECTIONS ▷ **Read each pair of words. If they mean almost the same thing, circle synonym. If they are opposites, circle antonym.**

1.   long/short

synonym   antonym

2.   tired/sleepy

synonym   antonym

3.   mad/angry

synonym   antonym

4.   funny/boring

synonym   antonym

5.   loud/quiet

synonym   antonym

6.   pretty/cute

synonym   antonym

7.   angry/calm

synonym   antonym

8.   poor/rich

synonym   antonym

Homographs

Homographs are words that are spelled alike but have different meanings. Some homographs are pronounced differently.

Examples:

<u>felt</u>: a soft kind of cloth   <u>wind</u>: moving air

<u>felt</u>: sensed on the skin   <u>wind</u>: to turn a knob

DIRECTIONS   Look at each pair of pictures. Read each sentence. Then, write the letter of the correct meaning on the line.

bat

a.   b.

_____ **1.** Tony has a wooden bat.

_____ **2.** The bat sleeps during the day.

_____ **3.** The bat broke when Alberto hit the ball.

pitcher

a.   b.

_____ **7.** I put some juice in the pitcher.

_____ **8.** The pitcher threw the ball too low.

_____ **9.** The milk pitcher was empty.

plant

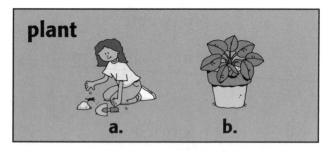

a.   b.

_____ **4.** Kendra wants to plant a tree.

_____ **5.** The farmer will plant his crops in the fall.

_____ **6.** Jody grew a plant at school.

light

a.   b.

_____ **10.** I will turn on the light.

_____ **11.** The feather is light.

_____ **12.** There is only one light in my room.

Homophones

Homophones are words that sound the same but are spelled differently.

Use <u>hear</u> to mean "to listen to."

Example:

    We <u>hear</u> the bell ringing.

Use <u>here</u> to mean "to this place" or "at this place."

Example:

    Bring the ticket <u>here</u>.

Use <u>your</u> when you mean "belonging to you."

Example:

    Do you have <u>your</u> homework?

Use <u>you're</u> when you mean "you are."

Example:

    <u>You're</u> in trouble now.

> **DIRECTIONS** — **Write <u>hear</u> or <u>here</u> to complete each sentence correctly.**

1. Did you _____ that the circus is coming?

2. Is it coming _____ soon?

3. Yes, it will be _____ today.

4. I think I _____ the music now.

> **DIRECTIONS** — **Write <u>your</u> or <u>you're</u> to complete each sentence correctly.**

5. _____ a good skater, Eric.

6. Pull _____ laces tight.

7. Now, _____ ready to skate safely.

8. Were _____ legs this wobbly when you started?

More Homophones

Remember, homophones are words that sound the same but are spelled differently.

Use <u>write</u> to mean "to put words on paper."

Example:

Please <u>write</u> your name on your paper.

Use <u>right</u> to mean "correct."

Example:

Your answer is <u>right</u>.

Use <u>right</u> to mean "the opposite of left."

Example:

Turn <u>right</u> to get to my school.

DIRECTIONS ⟩ **Write <u>right</u> or <u>write</u> to complete each sentence correctly.**

1. Chris likes to _____ on the board.

2. Everything was _____ on Martha's math paper.

3. We turn _____ to go to the lunchroom.

4. Our class is learning to _____ stories.

5. Kim drew the picture on the _____ side.

6. Luis can _____ in Spanish.

7. The teacher marked the _____ answers.

8. Be sure you do the _____ page.

9. Jenna will _____ about her birthday party.

10. James colors with his _____ hand.

Troublesome Words

Use <u>two</u> to mean "the number 2."

Example:

  <u>Two</u> children worked together.

Use <u>too</u> to mean "more than enough."

Example:

  There are <u>too</u> many people on the bus.

Use <u>too</u> to mean "also."

Example:

  May I help, <u>too</u>?

Use <u>to</u> to mean "toward" or "to do something."

Example:

  Let's go <u>to</u> the library <u>to</u> find Kim.

⦿⦿⦿⦿⦿⦿⦿⦿⦿⦿⦿⦿⦿⦿⦿⦿⦿⦿⦿⦿⦿⦿⦿⦿⦿⦿⦿⦿⦿⦿⦿⦿

DIRECTIONS ➤ **Write <u>two</u>, <u>too</u>, or <u>to</u> to complete each sentence.**

1. The children were working _____ make a class library.

2. Andy had _____ books in his hand.

3. He gave them _____ Ms. Diaz.

4. Ms. Diaz was happy _____ get the books.

5. "We can never have _____ many books," she said.

6. Rosa said she would bring _____ or three books.

7. James wanted to bring some, _____ .

8. Joann found a book that was _____ old.

9. Pages started _____ fall out when she picked it up.

10. Soon, everyone would have new books _____ read.

11. We can take out _____ of these books at a time.

More Troublesome Words

Use <u>there</u> when you mean "in that place."
Example:
> The dinosaur is over <u>there</u>.

Use <u>their</u> when you mean "belonging to them."
Example:
> This is <u>their</u> swamp.

<u>They're</u> is a contraction for <u>they are</u>. Use <u>they're</u> when you mean "they are."
Example:
> <u>They're</u> eating leaves from the trees.

DIRECTIONS Circle the correct word in ( ) to complete each sentence.

1. Is this (their, they're) food?

2. (There, They're) huge animals.

3. A big one is over (there, their).

4. Once it was (there, their) land.

5. Dinosaurs lived (they're, there) for a while.

6. (They're, There) everywhere!

7. (They're, There) the two biggest dinosaurs.

8. The faster dinosaur is resting (their, there).

9. Small dinosaurs lived (they're, there) long ago.

10. (Their, There) land was different then.

11. I see some more dinosaurs over (they're, there).

12. (They're, There) in the lake.

Compound Words

Sometimes two words can be put together to make a new word. The new word is called a **compound word**.

Examples:

    lunch + room = lunchroom

    every + day = everyday

 DIRECTIONS ➤ Write compound words. Pick words from Box 1 and Box 2. Write the new word in Box 3.

	Box 1	Box 2	Box 3
1.	sun	noon	_____
2.	after	glasses	_____
3.	play	side	_____
4.	birth	ground	_____
5.	out	book	_____
6.	scrap	day	_____

DIRECTIONS ➤ Write a compound word to finish each sentence. You may use the compound words you made above.

7. Dana was wearing _____ in class.

8. In the _____, Dana was sent to the principal's office.

9. Brad put a picture of the school in his _____.

10. Brad will be eight years old on his next _____.

11. We can't go _____ if it rains.

12. The _____ will be too wet.

More Compound Words

Remember, sometimes two words can be put together to make a compound word.
Example:

sun + flower = sunflower

DIRECTIONS Draw a line between two words that make a compound word.

1. snow   rope
2. rail   ball
3. rain   bow
4. sail   road
5. jump   boat
6. ear   plane
7. air   ring

DIRECTIONS Write three sentences using three of the words you made.

8. _____

_____

9. _____

_____

10. _____

_____

Prefixes

A **prefix** is a group of letters added to the beginning of a word.
Adding a prefix to a word changes its meaning.
Example:

The old woman was <u>happy</u>.
The old woman was <u>unhappy</u>.

Prefix	Meaning	Example
un	not	<u>un</u>clear
re	again	<u>re</u>write

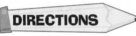 **DIRECTIONS** ▷ **Read each sentence. Underline the word that has a prefix. Tell the meaning of the word.**

1. The old man was unable to find something to wear.

_____

2. The old woman reopened the drawer.

_____

3. She told the old man they were unlucky.

_____

4. The old man felt this was unfair.

_____

5. He was very unhappy.

_____

6. The woman asked the man to rewind the yarn.

_____

7. The old woman rewashed the socks.

_____

8. Could the socks be uneven?

_____

9. The old man refilled his wife's glass.

_____

10. The farmer's wife reknitted the sweater.

_____

Suffixes

A **suffix** is a group of letters added to the end of a word. Adding a suffix to a word changes its meaning.

Example:

Josef's parents were <u>helpless</u>.
The doctor was <u>helpful</u>.

Suffix	Meaning	Example
ful	full of	hope<u>ful</u>
less	without	use<u>less</u>
able	able to be	break<u>able</u>

DIRECTIONS Read each sentence. Underline the word that has a suffix. Tell the meaning of the word.

1. Is Josef careful? _____

2. Josef thought the game was harmless. _____

3. The chair Josef was on was breakable. _____

DIRECTIONS Complete each sentence with a word from the box. Tell the meaning of the word you chose.

hopeful	dreadful	thankful

4. Josef's parents had a _____ shock!

_____

5. They were _____ the chair would not break.

_____

6. When Josef came out of the hospital, he was very _____.

_____

Writing Sentences

Remember, sentences have a naming part and an action part.
Example:

Naming Part	Action Part
Sara	won the race.

DIRECTIONS Draw a line from a naming part to an action part to make sentences.

Naming Part	Action Part
1. Grandma	baked
2. Aunt Sue	sings
3. My friend	skates
4. Earl's dad	reads
5. Kiko's mom	cooks
6. Jon's sister	played

DIRECTIONS Write sentences with the naming parts and action parts you put together. Add some words of your own.

7. _____

8. _____

9. _____

10. _____

11. _____

12. _____

Practice with Writing Sentences

Remember, sentences have a naming part and an action part.

DIRECTIONS Read each sentence. Circle the naming part. Underline the action part.

1. My sister sings.

2. My brother dances.

3. They perform.

4. People clap.

DIRECTIONS Rewrite each sentence, adding some words of your own.

5. My sister sings.

_____

6. My brother dances.

_____

7. They perform.

_____

8. People clap.

_____

Paragraphs

A **paragraph** is a group of sentences that tells about one main idea. The first line of a paragraph is indented. This means the first word is moved in a little from the left margin.

The first sentence in a paragraph often tells the main idea. The other sentences tell about the main idea.

Example:

      A safe home keeps people from getting hurt. Shoes or toys should not be left on the stairs. Matches, medicines, and cleaners should be locked safely away. Grown-ups should get things that are on high shelves instead of letting children reach for them. Then, children will not fall and get hurt.

How to Write a Paragraph

1. Write a sentence that tells the main idea.
2. Indent the first line.
3. Write sentences that tell more about the main idea.

DIRECTIONS → **Write three sentences that tell about this main idea.**

There are many things you can do to be safe at school.

_____

_____

_____

_____

_____

Main Idea

The **main idea** of a paragraph is often in the first sentence. It tells what the paragraph is about.
Example:

I have nice neighbors. Ms. Hill gives me flowers. Mr. Stone always smiles and waves. Miss Higgins plays ball with me.

ⓞⓞⓞⓞⓞⓞⓞⓞⓞⓞⓞⓞⓞⓞⓞⓞⓞⓞⓞⓞⓞⓞⓞⓞⓞⓞⓞⓞⓞⓞⓞⓞⓞⓞ

DIRECTIONS ▷ **Read each paragraph. Write the sentence that tells the main idea.**

Uncle Joe is a funny man. He tells jokes about elephants. He does magic tricks that don't work. He makes funny faces when he tells stories. He always makes me laugh.

1. _____

_____

Dad told us a funny story about his dog. When Dad was a little boy, he had a dog named Tiger. One day, Dad forgot his lunch. Dad said Tiger would bring it to school. A friend thought it would be a real tiger.

2. _____

_____

Firefighters are brave people. They go into burning buildings. They put out fires. They teach families how to be safe in their homes.

3. _____

_____

ⓞⓞⓞⓞⓞⓞⓞⓞⓞⓞⓞⓞⓞⓞⓞⓞⓞⓞⓞⓞⓞⓞⓞⓞⓞⓞⓞⓞⓞⓞ

Practice with the Main Idea

Remember, the main idea of a paragraph is often in the first sentence. It tells what the paragraph is about.

DIRECTIONS → **Read each paragraph. Write the sentence that tells the main idea.**

Making pasta is easy. First, you have to boil water. Add a little salt and oil. Let the water boil. Put the pasta in the water until it gets soft. Drain the noodles through a special bowl with holes in the bottom. Put your pasta on a plate and enjoy!

1. _____

_____

My mom is a very busy person. She works at a library. She coaches our swim team. She does all of the shopping. She helps Dad cook dinner. She reads to us every night. She even exercises after we go to bed.

2. _____

_____

Having a dog is fun, but it is also a lot of work. You have to remember to feed and walk the dog. You have to train it. Sometimes you have to play with it, even if you are tired. You have to wash and brush it. You have to clean up after it. It's a good thing that dogs are cute!

3. _____

_____

Supporting Details

The other sentences in a paragraph give details about the main idea in the beginning sentence.

Example:

I have nice neighbors. **Ms. Hill gives me flowers. Mr. Stone always smiles and waves. Miss Higgins plays ball with me.**

DIRECTIONS Read each paragraph. Circle the main idea. Underline the sentences that give details about the main idea.

1. Uncle Joe is a funny man. He tells jokes about elephants. He does magic tricks that don't work. He makes funny faces when he tells stories. He always makes me laugh.

2. Dad told us a funny story about his dog. When Dad was a little boy, he had a dog named Tiger. One day Dad forgot his lunch. Dad said Tiger would bring it to school. A friend thought it would be a real tiger.

3. Firefighters are brave people. They go into burning buildings. They put out fires. They teach families how to be safe in their homes.

Practice with Supporting Details

Remember, the main idea tells what a paragraph is about. The other sentences in a paragraph give details about the main idea.

DIRECTIONS ➤ **Read each paragraph. Circle the main idea. Underline the sentences that give details about the main idea.**

1.   Making pasta is easy. First, you have to boil water. Add a little salt and oil. Let the water boil. Put the pasta in the water until it gets soft. Drain the noodles through a special bowl with holes in the bottom. Put your pasta on a plate and enjoy!

2.   My mom is a very busy person. She works at a library. She coaches our swim team. She does all of the shopping. She helps Dad cook dinner. She reads to us every night. She even exercises after we go to bed.

3.   Having a dog is fun, but it is also a lot of work. You have to remember to feed and walk the dog. You have to train it. Sometimes you have to play with it, even if you are tired. You have to wash and brush it. You have to clean up after it. It's a good thing that dogs are cute!

Order in Paragraphs

The sentences in a paragraph tell things in the order in which they happened.

Words such as <u>first</u>, <u>second</u>, <u>third</u>, <u>next</u>, <u>then</u>, and <u>last</u> can help tell when things happened.

Examples:

Jane got ready for bed. **First**, she took a bath. **Next**, she brushed her teeth. **Then**, she put on her pajamas. **Last**, she read a story and got into bed.

> **DIRECTIONS** Write *1, 2, 3,* or *4* to show what happened first, second, third, and last.

Eva planted flowers. First, she got a shovel. Next, she dug some holes in the garden. Then, she put the flowers into the holes. Last, she put the shovel back in its place.

_____ Then, she put the flowers into the holes.

_____ Next, she dug some holes in the garden.

_____ Last, she put the shovel back in its place.

_____ First, she got a shovel.

Dan and Larry washed the car. First, they got the car wet. Next, they put soap all over it. Then, they washed all the soap off. Last, they dried the car.

_____ They put soap all over the car.

_____ They washed all the soap off.

_____ Dan and Larry dried the car.

_____ The boys got the car wet.

Practice with Order in Paragraphs

Remember, the sentences in a paragraph tell things in the order in which they happened.

Words such as <u>first</u>, <u>second</u>, <u>third</u>, <u>next</u>, <u>then</u>, and <u>last</u> can help tell when things happened.

DIRECTIONS ➤ **Write *1*, *2*, *3*, or *4* to show what happened first, second, third, and last.**

Have you ever made instant pudding? In a bowl, stir the pudding mix with 2 cups of cold milk. Next, pour the pudding into cups. Then, chill the pudding for five minutes. Finally, enjoy the yummy treat.

_____ Finally, enjoy the yummy treat.

_____ In a bowl, stir the pudding mix with 2 cups of cold milk.

_____ Then, chill the pudding for five minutes.

_____ Next, pour the pudding into cups.

Learning to swim took a long time. First, I had to get used to the water. Then, I had to learn to float. Next, my teacher taught me a swimming stroke. Finally, I was ready to try on my own.

_____ Next, my teacher taught me a swimming stroke.

_____ Then, I had to learn to float.

_____ Finally, I was ready to try on my own.

_____ First, I had to get used to the water.

Personal Narrative

A **personal narrative** is a story about the writer. In a story, a writer tells about one main idea. Every story has a beginning, a middle, and an ending.

Example:

> One day my grandfather and I went to the zoo. First, we looked at lions and tigers. Next, we watched the monkeys play. Then, we went to see the bears. Last, Grandfather helped me feed the seals. My day with Grandfather was wonderful!

How to Write a Paragraph About Yourself

1. Write a sentence that tells about something that happened to you. Tell where the story took place.
2. Write sentences that tell about what happened in order. Use the words <u>first</u>, <u>next</u>, <u>then</u>, and <u>last</u>.
3. Tell how the story ended.
4. Use the words <u>I</u> and <u>me</u>.
5. Give the story a title.

DIRECTIONS Read the example paragraph above. Answer the questions.

1. Where does the story take place?

_____

2. What happens after they look at the lions and tigers?

_____

3. What happens last?

_____

Personal Narrative

Practice with Personal Narrative

DIRECTIONS > **Finish the paragraph. Add words that tell about yourself.**

I had a good day at school. First, I _____

_____. Next, I _____

_____. Then, I ate lunch with my friend

_____.

Last, I _____

_____.

DIRECTIONS > **Use the chart to write a story about yourself.**

Beginning	Middle	Ending
Who is in the story? Where does the story happen?	What happens?	How do things work out?

_____

_____

_____

_____

_____

_____

_____

_____

Poem

In a **poem**, a writer paints a picture with words. Many poems have rhyming words at the end of every line or every other line.

Example:

Special Things

I like
White snow and blue bows.
I like
The sweet red rose.
I like
The crunchy sand between my toes.
I like
My puppy's wet, black nose.

How to Write a Poem

1. End some lines with rhyming words.
2. Try to paint a picture with words.
3. Give your poem a title.

 DIRECTIONS Read the example poem above. Answer the questions.

1. What is the poem about?

_____

2. Name two rhyming words in the poem.

_____

3. Name two words that describe in the poem.

_____

Practice with Poems

Finish this poem. Think of describing words and words that rhyme. Give your poem a title.

_____

Summer is fun.

I can _____.

I feel so free

Like a ___._____.

DIRECTIONS Finish the chart. Use the chart to write a poem.

My title
_____

Describing words I will use	Rhyming words I will use
_____	_____
_____	_____
_____	_____
_____	_____

_____

_____

_____

_____

Describing Paragraph

In a paragraph that **describes**, a writer tells about a person, place, or thing. The sentences have describing words that help the reader see, hear, taste, smell, and feel.

Example:

Many birds visit my backyard. Red cardinals make nests in our bushes. Tiny hummingbirds buzz around the yellow flowers in our garden. Robins chirp sweetly and wake me in the morning.

How to Write a Paragraph That Describes

1. Write a sentence that tells whom or what the paragraph is about.
2. Write sentences that tell more about the main idea.
3. Use describing words in your sentences.

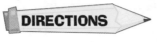 **DIRECTIONS** > **Read the example describing paragraph. Answer the questions.**

1. What is the topic of the paragraph?

_____

2. Which words tell what the birds are like?

_____

3. Write a describing sentence to add to the paragraph.

_____

Describing Paragraph, page 2

Finish the paragraph. Add describing words.

The little woman put on her _____ hat.

She went outside. It was a _____ day. The sky was

_____. The little woman felt _____.

Finish the chart. Write describing words about your topic. Use the chart to write a describing paragraph.

My topic:				
Looks	**Feels**	**Tastes**	**Smells**	**Sounds**
_____	_____	_____	_____	_____
_____	_____	_____	_____	_____
_____	_____	_____	_____	_____
_____	_____	_____	_____	_____

_____

_____

_____

_____

_____

_____

_____

Friendly Letter

A **friendly letter** is a letter you write to someone you know.
A friendly letter has five parts. They are the heading, greeting, body, closing, and signature.
Example:

heading — October 22, 2005

greeting — Dear Grandma,

body — The sweater you knitted for my birthday is great! The fall days here have been chilly. It's nice to have a new, warm sweater to wear. It is just the right size. Thank you, Grandma.

closing — Love,

signature — Emily

How to Write a Friendly Letter
1. Choose a friend or a relative to write to.
2. Write about things you have done.
3. Be sure your letter has a heading, greeting, body, closing, and signature.
4. Use capital letters and commas correctly.

DIRECTIONS > Read the example friendly letter. Answer the questions.

1. Whom did Emily write the letter to?

_____

2. Why did Emily write the letter?

_____

Friendly Letter, page 2

heading _____

greeting _____

body _____

_____

_____

_____

_____

_____

_____

_____

_____

closing _____

signature _____

Envelopes

An **envelope** is used to send a letter or a note.
Example:

Mary Jo Wood
13 West Street — **return address**   **stamp**
Chicago, Illinois 60648

Mrs. May Williams
13 River Bend Road — **mailing address**
Crystal Lake, Illinois 60014

How to Address an Envelope
1. In the mailing address, tell who is receiving the letter.
2. In the return address, tell who is sending the letter.
3. Put a stamp on the envelope.

DIRECTIONS   **Think of someone you want to write to. Use the organizer below to address your envelope.**

How-to Paragraph

In a **how-to paragraph**, a writer tells how to make or do something. The steps are told in order.

Example:

Here is how to make a bird feeder. You will need a pine cone, string, peanut butter, and birdseed. First, tie the string to the top of the pine cone. Next, roll the pine cone in peanut butter. Then, roll the pine cone in birdseed. Last, go outside and tie the pine cone to a tree branch.

How to Write a How-to Paragraph
1. Write a sentence that tells what the paragraph is about.
2. Write a sentence that lists things you need.
3. Tell how to do something in order.
4. Use the words <u>first</u>, <u>next</u>, <u>then</u>, and <u>last</u>.

DIRECTIONS **Read the example how-to paragraph. Answer the questions.**

1. What does the paragraph tell how to do?

_____

_____

2. What materials are needed?

_____

_____

How-to Paragraph, page 2

DIRECTIONS > **Put these sentences for a how-to paragraph in order. Write
1, 2, 3, or *4* to show the order of the steps.**

_____ Next, fill the can with water.   _____ Here is how to water a plant.

_____ Last, water the plant.   _____ First, get a watering can.

DIRECTIONS > **Finish the chart. Use the chart to write a how-to paragraph.**

My topic: _____

Materials needed: _____

_____

_____

Steps:

1. _____

2. _____

3. _____

4. _____

_____

_____

_____

_____

_____

_____

Information Paragraph

In a paragraph that gives **information**, a writer gives facts and details about one topic.

Example:

> Many African American people celebrate Kwanzaa. It is a celebration of the customs and history of African American people. It is a gathering time for families, like Thanksgiving. The holiday is celebrated for seven days. It begins the day after Christmas. On each night of Kwanzaa, a candle is lit. Each candle stands for a rule to help people live their lives.

How to Write an Information Paragraph
1. Write a topic sentence. Tell who or what your paragraph is about.
2. Indent the first line.
3. Write detail sentences. Give interesting facts about the person, animal, place, or thing.

 Read the example information paragraph. Answer the questions.

1. What is the topic sentence of the information paragraph?

_____

_____

2. Write one detail sentence from the paragraph.

_____

_____

DIRECTIONS Think about a topic you would like to write about. Complete the chart. Use the chart to write an information paragraph.

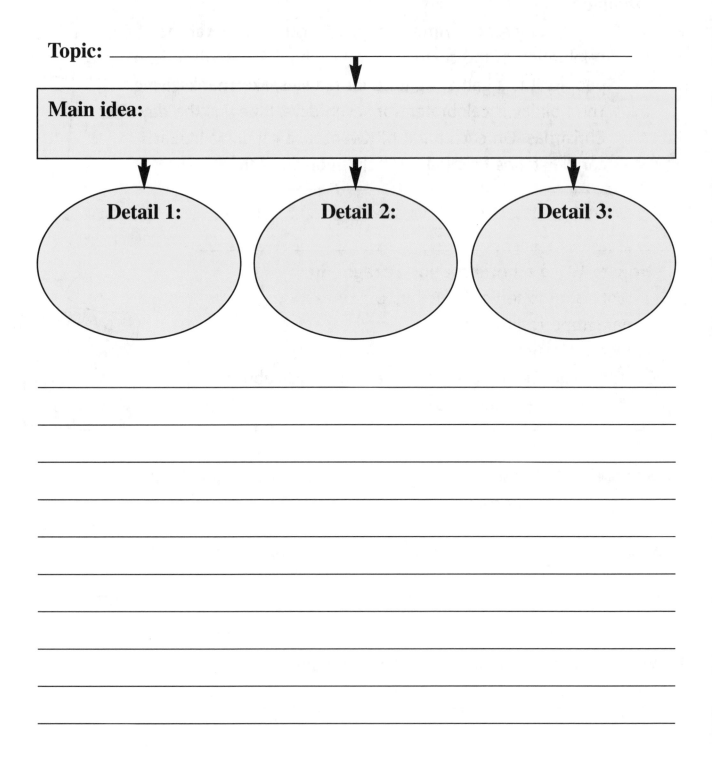

Topic: _____

Main idea:

Detail 1:

Detail 2:

Detail 3:

_____

_____

_____

_____

_____

_____

_____

_____

Book Report

A **book report** tells about a book. It also tells what you think about the book.

Example:

Title	<u>The Koala</u>
Author	Anita Best

About the Book   This book is about koalas. It tells many facts about this animal. Here are some of them. Koalas live in Australia. They live in trees. They eat leaves.

What I Think   This is a good book. I learned many things about koalas.

How to Write a Book Report
1. Write the title of the book. Underline it.
2. Write the author's name.
3. Tell some facts about the book. Tell about important people, places, and things in the book.
4. Tell what you think about the book.

DIRECTIONS   Read the example book report. Answer the questions.

1. What is the title of the book?

_____

2. Who wrote the book?

_____

3. What did the writer of the report think about the book?

_____

_____

Book Report, page 2

DIRECTIONS Think of a book you would like to tell about. Fill in the information at the top and use it to write a book report.

Title of book: _____

Author of book: _____

Facts about book: _____

_____

_____

Should others read this book? _____

DIRECTIONS Use the information above to write a book report.

_____

_____

_____

_____

_____

_____

_____

_____

_____

_____

Persuading Paragraph

> A **persuading paragraph** tries to make the reader agree with the writer's opinion.
>
> *Example*:
>
>> I think that a lizard should be our class pet. A lizard is small and easy to care for. It doesn't eat much food. Lizards are interesting to watch, too. Vote for the lizard!

How to Write a Persuading Paragraph
1. Write about something you feel strongly about.
2. Tell how you feel in the first sentence.
3. Give reasons why other people should feel the same way.
4. Ask your reader to do something in the last sentence.

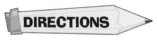 **DIRECTIONS** > **Read the example persuading paragraph. Answer the questions.**

1. What is the writer's opinion in the first sentence?

_____

2. What is one reason the writer gives to make the reader agree?

_____

_____

3. What does the writer want the reader to do?

_____

_____

Persuading Paragraph, page 2

DIRECTIONS ▷ Think of something you feel strongly about. Fill in the information at the top and use it to write a persuading paragraph.

Main idea: _____

Reason 1: _____

_____

Reason 2: _____

Reason 3 (your strongest reason): _____

_____

What the reader should do: _____

_____

_____

_____

_____

_____

_____

_____

_____

_____

_____

Words in ABC Order

The order of letters from <u>A</u> to <u>Z</u> is called **ABC order**, or **alphabetical order**.

When words begin with the same letter, the next letter of the word is used to put the words in ABC order: <u>c</u>ape, <u>c</u>hapel, <u>c</u>ity.

DIRECTIONS ▷ **Number the words in ABC order. Then, write the words in the correct order.**

1. _____ bat   1. _____

_____ air   2. _____

_____ cat   3. _____

5. _____ joke   1. _____

_____ lake   2. _____

_____ king   3. _____

2. _____ top   1. _____

_____ sea   2. _____

_____ rock   3. _____

6. _____ neck   1. _____

_____ owl   2. _____

_____ mail   3. _____

3. _____ egg   1. _____

_____ fish   2. _____

_____ dog   3. _____

7. _____ yes   1. _____

_____ zoo   2. _____

_____ walk   3. _____

4. _____ hat   1. _____

_____ ice   2. _____

_____ gate   3. _____

8. _____ pan   1. _____

_____ oak   2. _____

_____ nail   3. _____

Practice with ABC Order

Remember, when words begin with the same letter, the next letter in the word is used put the words in ABC order.
Example:
    ab̲out, an̲t, ap̲ple

Number the words in ABC order. Then, write the words in the correct order. Remember to look at the second letter in each word to help you.

1. _____ hop   1. _____
    _____ hat   2. _____
    _____ hill   3. _____

5. _____ bug   1. _____
    _____ back   2. _____
    _____ bring   3. _____

2. _____ fun   1. _____
    _____ four   2. _____
    _____ far   3. _____

6. _____ goat   1. _____
    _____ gate   2. _____
    _____ great   3. _____

3. _____ ten   1. _____
    _____ train   2. _____
    _____ top   3. _____

7. _____ snake 1. _____
    _____ sad   2. _____
    _____ star   3. _____

4. _____ art   1. _____
    _____ awful 2. _____
    _____ ate   3. _____

8. _____ plane 1. _____
    _____ pig   2. _____
    _____ prince 3. _____

Using a Dictionary

A **dictionary** is a book that lists words and their meanings. The words in a dictionary are listed in ABC order.

Words can be put in ABC order. The first letters of these words were used to put them in ABC order.

<u>f</u>lower

<u>g</u>arden

<u>h</u>ome

Many words on a dictionary page begin with the same letter. When words begin with the same letter, the second letter is used to put the words in ABC order.

s<u>e</u>eds

s<u>t</u>ory

s<u>u</u>n

DIRECTIONS Put each group of words in ABC order. Remember to use the second letter in each word if the first letter is the same.

1. noise _____

music _____

poem _____

3. garden _____

ground _____

frog _____

2. sun _____

rain _____

plant _____

4. afraid _____

asleep _____

alone _____

Using a Dictionary, page 2

Each word listed in the dictionary is called an **entry word**. Entry words are in ABC order.

The two words at the top of a dictionary page are called **guide words**. The word on the left is the first entry word on the page. The word on the right is the last entry word on the page. All the other entry words on the page are in ABC order between the first and the last words.

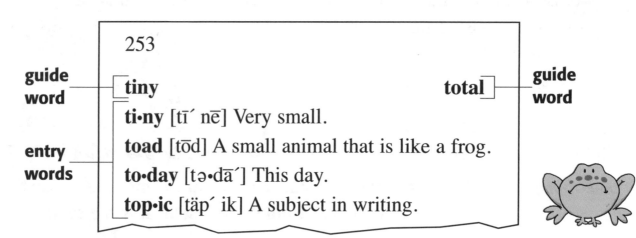

253

guide word — **tiny**   **total** — guide word

entry words —
ti·ny [tī′ nē] Very small.
toad [tōd] A small animal that is like a frog.
to·day [tə·dā′] This day.
top·ic [täp′ ik] A subject in writing.

DIRECTIONS   Use the dictionary page above. Answer these questions.

1. What is the first entry word on page 253? _____

2. Would you find the word <u>think</u> on this page? _____

3. What entry word tells about an animal? _____

4. What entry word means "very small"? _____

5. Could the entry word <u>together</u> be on this page? _____

Why or why not? _____

_____

Using a Dictionary, page 3

Some entry words have more than one meaning. Each meaning has a number.

The dictionary has sentences that show how to use the entry word.

bump [bump] **1** To knock against: The goblin <u>bumped</u> against the tree. **2** A part that sticks out: The goblin fell over a <u>bump</u> in the road.

burst [burst] **1** To break apart suddenly: The balloon <u>burst</u>. **2** To give way to a strong feeling: Grandfather and I <u>burst</u> into laughter.

DIRECTIONS ▷ **Read the dictionary entries. Answer the questions.**

1. What word can mean "to break apart"? _____

2. What is the example sentence for meaning 2 of <u>burst</u>?

_____

3. Which word can mean "to knock against"?

_____

4. What is the number of the meaning of <u>bump</u> in this sentence?

The goblin fell over a <u>bump</u> in the road.

_____

5. Write your own example sentences for each meaning of <u>bump</u> and <u>burst</u>.

_____

_____

Using a Dictionary, page 4

Use the dictionary words to answer the questions. Write <u>yes</u> or <u>no</u>.

always	at all times
animal	a living thing that is not a plant
bed	a place to sleep
dark	without light
green	the color of grass
hay	grass cut, dried, and used as food for cows and horses
hungry	needing food
kitten	a young cat
ladder	a set of steps used to climb up and down
library	a building where books are kept

1. Is <u>hay</u> something that alligators eat? _____

2. Is a <u>bed</u> a place for swimming? _____

3. Is grass <u>green</u>? _____

4. Is a flower an <u>animal</u>? _____

5. Can you use a <u>ladder</u> to climb to the roof? _____

6. Is a baby pig called a <u>kitten</u>? _____

7. Is a <u>library</u> a place for food? _____

8. Are you <u>hungry</u> after having lunch? _____

Using an Encyclopedia

An **encyclopedia** is a set of books that has facts on many subjects. Each book in a set is called a volume. The volumes list subjects in ABC order.

DIRECTIONS Use the model encyclopedia in the picture. Write the number of the volume in which you would find each of these subjects.

1. Ohio River _____

2. explorers _____

3. Rocky Mountains _____

4. cows _____

5. United States _____

6. farming _____

DIRECTIONS Write the word or words you would use to look up the following subjects in an encyclopedia.

7. pretty butterflies _____

8. kinds of dogs _____

9. trees in the United States _____

10. Florida history _____

Parts of a Book

The **title page** tells the title of a book. It gives the name of the author. The author is the person who wrote the book.

The **table of contents** lists the chapters or parts of the book. It tells the page where each chapter or part begins.

Some books have an **index**. It is in ABC order. It tells the pages where things can be found.

	Contents	Apartments, 2, 7
<u>Kinds of Houses</u> by Jack Builder	1. Brick Houses ....1 2. City Houses.................5 3. Country Houses.........8 4. Wood Houses..........15	Basements, 25 Ceilings, 2, 9 Concrete, 4, 16 Doors, 12, 17
title page	**table of contents**	**index**

DIRECTIONS — Look at the sample pages. Answer these questions.

1. What is the title of the book? _____

2. Who wrote the book? _____

3. How many chapters are in this book? _____

4. On what page does chapter 4 begin? _____

5. On which pages can you find facts about ceilings? _____

Parts of a Book, page 2

Remember, the title page is in the front of a book. It tells you the title of the book. It tells you who wrote the book. It tells you who drew (illustrated) the pictures in the book. And it tells you what company published the book.

DIRECTIONS ▶ Look at this title page from a book about cats. Then, write your answers to the questions below on the lines.

ALL ABOUT CATS
by
Patricia L. Keller

Illustrated by
Richard H. Green

Coaster Press
New York

1. What is the title of the book? _____

2. Who wrote the book? _____

3. Who illustrated the book? _____

4. What company published the book? _____

Parts of a Book, page 3

Remember, the table of contents is near the front of a book. It tells you what each chapter of the book is about. When you want to know what a book is about, you should read the table of contents.

DIRECTIONS → **Look at this page from the book <u>All About Cats</u>. Then, write the correct answers to the questions on the lines below.**

Table of Contents

1. What chapter tells you what to do if your cat gets sick? _____

2. What chapter tells you about different kinds of cats? _____

3. What page tells you how to pick the right cat? _____

4. What is the name of the chapter on page 27?

_____

Kinds of Books

Some books are called **fiction**. They are stories about make-believe people and things. Here are some titles of books that are fiction.

    Ask Mr. Bear

    The Bears Go to the Hospital

Nonfiction books tell about real people or things. Here are some of the titles of books that are nonfiction.

    The Hospital Book

    Who Keeps Us Safe?

A library has fiction and nonfiction books. The fiction books are in one part of the library. The nonfiction books are in another part.

DIRECTIONS   **Read about each book. Tell if the book is <u>fiction</u> or <u>nonfiction</u>.**

1. a book about a magic bear _____

2. a book that tells how to keep your home safe _____

3. a book that tells how to ride a bicycle safely _____

4. a book about a bear that can draw _____

5. a book about a house that can talk _____

6. a book about the fire department _____

7. a book about a dog that can fly _____

Kinds of Books, page 2

Remember, some books are called fiction. Fiction stories are about make-believe people or things.

Nonfiction books tell about real people or things.

A library has fiction and nonfiction books. The fiction books are in one part of the library. The nonfiction books are in another part.

DIRECTIONS Read about each book. Tell if the book is <u>fiction</u> or <u>nonfiction</u>.

1. a book about the first woman in space _____

2. a book about a cat that can talk _____

3. a book about types of plants _____

4. a book about a boy that can fly _____

DIRECTIONS Go to your bookshelf and find two fiction books and two nonfiction books. Write each title below. Then write <u>fiction</u> or <u>nonfiction</u> to show what kind of book each is.

5. _____ _____

6. _____ _____

7. _____ _____

8. _____ _____

Fact or Fantasy?

Some stories that you read tell you facts about things. They tell you what could really happen. You might read about how a kitten likes to chase a mouse. This is really true. It is a **fact**.

Some stories tell about things that could not happen. In these stories, animals may talk or act like people. People may do things that could not really happen. These stories are called **fantasy**. "Goldilocks and the Three Bears" is a fantasy. It could not really happen.

DIRECTIONS Read each sentence. Write <u>fact</u> by the sentences that are true. Write <u>fantasy</u> by the sentences that could not really happen.

_____ **1.** Some elephants live in the jungle.

_____ **2.** The elephant read three books today.

_____ **3.** The pig built a brick house.

_____ **4.** That monkey grabbed my hat!

_____ **5.** The chicken put on an apron and washed the dishes.

_____ **6.** The oven said, "The cake is done."

_____ **7.** A zookeeper takes care of animals.

_____ **8.** Annie put on her magic ring and disappeared.

Fact or Fantasy, page 2

Remember, a fact is something that is true. A story about something that really happened is a fact.

Some stories tell about things that could not happen. These stories are called fantasy.

DIRECTIONS **Read each sentence. Write <u>fact</u> by the sentences that are true. Write <u>fantasy</u> by the sentences that could not really happen.**

_____ **1.** This morning my dog made eggs and toast for

breakfast.

_____ **2.** A veterinarian takes care of sick animals.

_____ **3.** Plants need water and light to grow.

_____ **4.** We take a ride in a flying car.

_____ **5.** Learning to play the piano takes time and practice.

_____ **6.** Seals are great swimmers.

_____ **7.** My sister's hair changes colors while she sleeps.

_____ **8.** The hummingbird is a very small bird.

Answer Key

Unit 1

Page 6

Order may vary. **1.** apple, **2.** car, **3.** rug, **4.** bird, **5.** chair, **6.** girl, **7.** tree, **8.** boy, **9.** desk, **10.** truck, **11.** grass, **12.** pen, **13.** girl, apple, **14.** bird, tree, **15.** chair, desk, **16.** boy, chair, **17.** girl, truck

Page 7

1. sister, park, **2.** car, mother, **3.** dog, **4.** boy, birds, trees, **5.** playground, **6.** cat, slide; Chart: Person: sister, mother, boy; Place: park, playground; Thing: car, trees, slide; Animal: dog, birds, cat

Page 8

Order may vary. **1.** Bob's Bikes, **2.** Bridge Road, **3.** China, **4.** Elf Corn, **5.** Gabriel, **6.** Lindsey, **7.** New York City, **8.** Oregon, **9.** Pat Green, **10.** State Street, **11.** Hill's Store, **12.** Baker Street, **13.** Stone Library, **14.** Emily Fuller

Page 9

1. dog/Lassie, **2.** park/Central Park, **3.** city/Chicago, **4.** woman/Ms. Ward, **5.** school/Redbrook Elementary School, **6.** store/Fastmart Grocery Store, **7.–9.** Answers will vary.

Page 10

1. Where did Jack Sprat go?, **2.** Mary saw her friend Jill., **3.** Did Mr. or Mrs. Sprat go with them?, **4.** They met Ms. Muffet along the way., **5.–6.** Proper nouns will vary.

Page 11

1. Meg, Tim; **2.** Ms. Lee; **3.** Holly Green; **4.** Lucy; **5.** Mr. Roberts; **6.** Lucy; **7.–8.** Answers will vary.

Page 12

1. They walked along Main Street., **2.** My uncle drove through Indiana and Ohio., **3.** We went on a trip to Mexico., **4.–8.** Proper nouns will vary.

Page 13

1. Wednesday, **2.** February, **3.** Saturday, **4.** Thanksgiving, **5.–7.** Answers will vary.

Page 14

1. boys, **2.** girl, **3.** robe, **4.** stars, **5.** moon, **6.** house, **7.** door, **8.** treats, **9.** cats, **10.** dogs, **11.** owl, **12.** stars, **13.** trees, **14.** hands, **15.** song

Page 15

1. caps, **2.** chairs, **3.** girls, **4.** trees, **5.** flags, **6.** boys, **7.** seeds, **8.** carrots, **9.** peas, **10.** friends, **11.** gardens

Page 16

1. lunches, **2.** dresses, **3.** glasses, **4.** dishes, **5.** boxes, **6.** watches, **7.** foxes, **8.** benches, **9.** inches, **10.** brushes, **11.** buses, **12.** churches

Page 17

1. woman, **2.** men, **3.** child, **4.** feet, **5.** teeth, **6.** children, **7.** feet, **8.** teeth, **9.** men, **10.** women

Page 18

1. shelf, **2.** wives, **3.** elf, **4.** wolves, **5.-7.** Answers will vary.

Page 19

1. We, **2.** She or He, **3.** She or He, **4.** It, **5.** She or He, **6.** It, **7.** They, **8.** We, **9.** They, **10.** We

Page 20

We, She, They, They, He, I, It

Page 21

1. I, **2.** me, **3.** me, **4.** I, **5.** Susan and I, **6.** Tina and me, **7.** Tina and I, **8.** Susan and me

Page 22

1. We, **2.** us, **3.** We, **4.** us, **5.** us, **6.** We, **7.** us, **8.** We, **9.** us, **10.** we, **11.** We

Page 23

1. runs, **2.** kicks, **3.** breaks, **4.** looks, **5.** shakes, **6.** turns, **7.** runs, **8.** talks, **9.** sends, **10.** pays; **11.–15.** Answers may vary. **11.** The boy reads., **12.** The baby cries., **13.** The rabbit hops., **14.** The birds sing., **15.** The dogs bark.

Page 24

1. lives, **2.** walk, **3.** tells, **4.** waves, **5.** makes, **6.** laugh, **7.-10.** Answers will vary.

Page 25

1. skips, **2.** play, **3.** hug, **4.** purrs, **5.** barks, **6.** hide, **7.** waves, **8.** blows, **9.** follows, **10.** sees, **11.** hears, **12.** move, **13.** hoots, **14.** take, **15.** eat

Page 26

1. The following verbs should be circled: reads, takes, rests, sleeps, snores, guess, practice, **2.** skates, **3.** wears, **4.** teaches, **5.** learn; **6.** practice, **7.** comes, **8.** claps, performs

Page 27

1. have, **2.** have, **3.** had, **4.** has, **5.** has, **6.** has, **7.** have, **8.** had, **9.** has, **10.** have, **11.** have, **12.** had

Page 28

1. are, **2.** are, **3.** were, **4.** is, **5.** are, **6.** were, **7.** is, **8.** am, **9.** was, **10.** is

Page 29

1. plays, **2.** runs, **3.** dance, **4.** wait, **5.** leaps; Paragraph (Answers may vary.): takes; sits; asks; dances; stands; walks

Page 30

1. paints, **2.** uses, **3.** hang, **4.** look, **5.** say, **6.-9.** Answers will vary.

Page 31

1. played, **2.** visited, **3.** looked, **4.** jumped, **5.** leaned, **6.** helped, **7.** laughed, **8.** The girls played in the park., **9.** They climbed over rocks., **10.** Their fathers called to them.

Page 32

1. wanted, **2.** baked, **3.** walked, **4.** signed, **5.** picked, **6.** surprised, **7.** looked, **8.–11.** Answers will vary.

Page 33

1. ran, **2.** came, **3.** went, **4.** go, **5.** run, **6.** goes, **7.** goes, went, **8.** comes, came, **9.** come, came, **10.** run, ran

Page 34

1. brought; **2.** fell; **3.** did; **4.** flew; **5.** broke; **6.** sold; **7.** ate; **8.** flies, flew; **9.** breaks, broke; **10.** does, did

Page 35

1. played, **2.** called, **3.** wanted, **4.** laughed, **5.** jumped, **6.** played, **7.** laughing, **8.** playing, **9.** talking, **10.** Carmen helped Grandma cook yesterday., **11.** Grandma is cooking some soup today.

Page 36

1. are, **2.** is, **3.** are, **4.** is, **5.** are, **6.** are, **7.** are, **8.** are; **9.–10.** Sentences will vary.

Page 37

1. is, **2.** are, **3.** are, **4.** are, **5.** is, **6.** is, **7.** are, **8.** are, **9.–10.** Answers will vary.

Page 38

1. were, **2.** was, **3.** were, **4.** were, **5.** were, **6.** was, **7.** was, **8.** were; **9.–10.** Sentences will vary.

Page 39

1. The following verbs should be circled: were, were, was, were, was, was, were, were, were, were.; **2.** Answers will vary.

Page 40

1. sees, **2.** saw, **3.** sees, **4.** sees, **5.** saw, **6.** saw, **7.** see, **8.** saw, **9.** saw, **10.** see; **11.** saw; Last week we saw Lee., **12.** sees; Lee sees my painting now.

Page 41

1. ran; Horses ran wild long ago., **2.** run; A horse can run ten miles every day., **3.** run; Can you run as fast as a horse?, **4.** ran; Mandy ran in a race last week., **5.** runs; Carl runs home from school now., **6.** runs; Now Mandy runs after Carl., **7.** run; How far can you run?

Page 42

1. give, **2.** gave, **3.** gives, **4.** gave, **5.** gave, **6.** gave, **7.** gave, **8.** gave, **9.–11.** Sentences will vary.

Page 43

1. do, **2.** does, **3.** does, **4.** does, **5.** does, **6.** do, **7.** does, **8.** do, **9.** does, **10.** do, **11.–12.** Sentences will vary.

Page 44

1. had, **2.** has, **3.** have, **4.** have, **5.** has, **6.** had, **7.** has, **8.** has, **9.** have, **10.** had, **11.** had, **12.** has

Page 45

The following verbs should be circled: has, has, had, had, had, have.

Page 46

Answers may vary. **1.** pink, **2.** long, **3.** brown, **4.** round, **5.** juicy, **6.** tiny

Page 47

Answers will vary. **1.** tired, **2.** happy, **3.** many, **4.** one, **5.** hungry, **6.** some, **7.** three, **8.** sleepy

Page 48

2. brighter, **3.** tallest, **4.** fast, **5.** thicker, **6.** biggest, **7.** wider, **8.** oldest

Page 49

1. better, **2.** worst, **3.** best, **4.** worse, **5.** better, **6.** best

Page 50

1. an, **2.** a, **3.** a, **4.** an, **5.** a, **6.** an, **7.** an, **8.** an, **9.** a, **10.** a, **11.** an, **12.** a, **13.** an, **14.** an, **15.** a, **16.** a, **17.** a, **18.** an, **19.** an, **20.** an, **21.** a, **22.** a

Page 51

In the column for **an**: ape, owl, eel, iguana, otter, ant; In the column for **a**: dog, butterfly, lizard, turtle, snake, bear

Unit 2

Page 52

1. no, **2.** yes, **3.** no, **4.** yes, **5.** yes, **6.** yes, **7.** no, **8.** no, **9.** yes, **10.** yes, **11.** yes, **12.** no, **13.** yes, **14.** no, **15.** yes

Page 53

Answers may vary. **1.** Mrs. Brown lives on my street., **2.** Our building is made of wood., **3.** Four families live in our building., **4.** Our class went on a picnic., **5.** Jennifer was climbing the tree., **6.** The sun shone all day., **7.** Corn and beans grow on a farm., **8.** The wagon has a broken wheel., **9.** The mother goat fed the baby goat., **10.** The boat sailed in strong winds., **11.** The fisherman caught seven fish., **12.** Some of the fish were sold in the store., **13.** Our team won ten games., **14.** Our batters hit the ball a lot., **15.** The ballpark was full of fans., **16.** Sentences will vary.

Page 54

Answers will vary.

Page 55

The following parts of each sentence should be circled: **1.** My family and I, **2.** Sami Harper, **3.** Miss Jenkins, **4.** Mr. Chang, **5.** Henry, **6.** Mr. Byrne,

7. Mrs. Lee, **8.** Mr. and Mrs. Diaz, **9.** Jeanine, **10.** Mr. Wolf, **11.** Amy Taft, **12.** Mr. Dowd, **13.** Mrs. Clark, **14.** Carolyn and Alberto, **15.** Julie

Page 56

1. fly, **2.** buzz, **3.** barks, **4.** quack, **5.** hops, **6.** roar, **7.** moo, **8.** cluck, **9.** Sentences will vary.

Page 57

1. My brother eats apples., **2.** Elizabeth drinks milk., **3.** Kim likes peanut butter., **4.** Justin wants bread., **5.** Chris plants corn., **6.** Chang caught a fish., **7.** Dad cooks breakfast., **8.** Shawn shares his lunch., **9.** Rosa grew the carrot.

Page 58

1. telling, **2.** telling, **3.** asking, **4.** not a sentence, **5.** telling, **6.** not a sentence, **7.** telling, **8.** asking, **9.** telling

Page 59

1. statement, **2.** question, **3.** statement, **4.** question, **5.** statement, **6.** question, **7.** exclamation, **8.** statement, **9.** question, **10.** exclamation

Page 60

Sentences will vary. Be sure each sentence is the specified type of sentence.

Page 61

1. John gave seeds to Sara and told her to plant them., **2.** Sara planted the seeds and looked at the ground., **3.** Sara sang songs and read stories to them., **4.** The rain fell on the seeds and helped them grow.

Page 62

1. The farmer and his family stood in the doorway., **2.** The hunter and the bear stayed with the family., **3.** The mice and the children ran out the door., **4.** The hunter and the bear went home.

Page 63

Answers will vary. Be sure each new sentence contains describing words.

Page 64

Answers used to fill in the story will vary but should all be adjectives.

Page 65

1. The ant climbed down a blade of grass. He (or She) fell into the spring., **2.** The bird pulled off a leaf. He (or She) let the leaf fall into the water., **3.** The hunter saw a lion. He spread his net., **4.** The lion and I live in the woods. We are friends.

Page 66

1. We were doing a project on volcanoes. **2.** They were doing a project on bees. **3.** She is a nice teacher. **4.** We all wanted to win. **5.** They were writing notes. **6.** She told everyone that Robert and Adam had won first prize.

Page 67

Answers will vary. Possible responses: **1.** stroll, **2.** race, **3.** pedal, **4.** speed, **5.** zooms, **6.** jogs, **7.** skip, **8.** travels, **9.** sails

Unit 3

Page 68

1. Mark Twain, **2.** Beverly Cleary, **3.** Diane Dillon, **4.** Alicia Acker, **5.** Ezra Jack Keats; The first letter of these words should be circled: **6.** mother, grandma, **7.** grandma, grandpa, **8.** uncle carlos, aunt kathy, **9.** Mario Martinez told me a story., **10.** Ichiro and I played ball.

Page 69

1. C.D., **2.** C.A.C., **3.** M.B., **4.** M.T., **5.** K.S., **6.** T.L.T., **7.** I.B., **8.** C.L.W., **9.** J.W.A., **10.** L.B. Hopkins, **11.** A. Martinez, **12.** Patricia A. Rosen, **13.** The box was for M. S. Mills., **14.** D. E. Ellis sent it to her., **15.** T. J. Lee brought the box to the house.

Page 70

1. Mrs. Ruth Scott, 2. Mr. Kurt Wiese, 3. Miss E. Garcia, 4. Dr. Seuss, 5. Ms. Carol Baylor, 6. Mr. and Mrs. H. Cox, 7. Miss K. E. Jones, 8. Dr. S. Tomas Rios, 9. Mrs. H. Stone is here to see Dr. Brooks., 10. Mr. F. Green and Ms. Miller are not here.

Page 71

1. James lives in Dayton, Ohio., 2. His house is on Market St., 3. I think Thomas Park is in this town., 4. We went to Mathis Lake for a picnic. 5. Is Perry School far away?

Page 72

1.–6. Answers will vary.

Page 73

1. Monday, 2. Friday, 3. February, 4. Answers will vary., 5. November, 6. Tues., 7. Thurs., 8. Dec., 9. Sat., 10. Jan., 11. Sept.

Page 74

1. New Year's Day, 2. Mother's Day, 3. Independence Day, 4. Labor Day, 5. Cinco de Mayo, 6. Thanksgiving Day, 7. Veterans Day, 8. Earth Day is in April., 9. Boxing Day is a British holiday., 10. Father's Day is in June.

Page 75

1. Best Friends, 2. The Biggest Bear, 3. Rabbits on Roller Skates, 4. Down on the Sunny Farm; The first letter of these words should be circled: 5. we, bees, 6. the, dancing, pony, 7. my, shadow, 8. my, summer, farm

Page 76

1. My mom's favorite book is called Gone with the Wind. 2. Alison wrote a poem named "Hay Is for Horses." 3. At the library, I checked out a book called Learn to Draw. 4. I read a story about boats called "Sail Away." 5. Mrs. Gibbs read us a poem named "A Plan for Stan." 6. Sara wrote a story called "What I Did on Vacation." 7. Her favorite book is called Ramona the Great.

Page 77

The first letter in each sentence should be capitalized.

Page 78

1. Patty played on the baseball team., 2. Patty hit two home runs., 3. She caught the ball, too., 4. What time is it?, 5. Is it time for lunch?, 6. Are you ready to eat?

Page 79

1.–5. Each sentence should end with a period., 6. Ms., 7. Mr., 8. Mrs., 9. Dr., 10. Ms.

Page 80

1. !, 2. ?, 3. ?, 4. !, 5. don't, 6. I'll, 7. didn't

Page 81

1. ?, 2. ?, 3. !, 4. ?, 5. One thing I don't like is setting up the tent., 6. I can't seem to get it right!, 7. I'll ask my mom for help next time.

Page 82

1. were not, weren't; 2. was not, wasn't; 3. has not, hasn't; 4. have not, haven't; 5. did not, didn't; 6. are not, aren't; 7. is not; 8. do not; 9. was not; 10. can not; 11. did not; 12. had not; 13. does not; 14. are not; 15. isn't; 16. don't; 17. didn't

Page 83

1. don't, 2. can't, 3. haven't, 4. doesn't, 5. isn't, 6.–8. Answers will vary.

Page 84

June 8, 2005 / Dear Grandmother, / The tag says it comes from Chicago, Illinois. / Love,

Page 85

1. Akron, Ohio, 2. Hilo, Hawaii, 3. Macon, Georgia, 4. Nome, Alaska, 5. Provo, Utah, 6. Nancy lives in Barnet, Vermont., 7. Mr. Hill went to Houston, Texas., 8. Did Bruce like Bend, Oregon?, 9. Will Amy visit Newark, Ohio?, 10. How far away is Salem, Massachusetts?

Page 86

1. Dec. 12, 1948, 2. Mar. 27, 1965, 3. Sept. 8, 1994, 4. Nov. 1, 2000, 5. Jan. 5, 1995, 6. August 10, 1967, 7. Oct. 17, 1983, 8. February 8, 1991, 9. July 29, 1989, 10. Sept. 3, 2001, 11. Oct. 20, 1988, 12. Answers will vary.

Unit 4

Page 87

1. hat, 2. bee, 3. cow, 4. dog

Page 88

1. dog/hog, 2. tall/ball, 3. mouse/house, 4. flat/hat, 5. blue/clue, 6. Rhymes will vary.

Page 89

1. road, 2. home, 3. sad, 4. sick, 5. gift, 6. small, 7. large, 8. dog, 9. yell, 10. great, 11. dad, 12. sleep

Page 90

1. soft, 2. long, 3. dark, 4. on, 5. happy, 6. low, 7. dry, 8. slow, 9. bad, 10. cold, 11. go, 12. hard

Page 91

1. antonym, 2. synonym, 3. synonym, 4. antonym, 5. antonym, 6. synonym, 7. antonym, 8. antonym

Page 92

1. a, 2. b, 3. a, 4. a, 5. a, 6. b, 7. b, 8. a, 9. b, 10. a, 11. b, 12. a

Page 93

1. hear, 2. here, 3. here, 4. hear, 5. You're, 6. your, 7. you're, 8. your

Page 94

1. write, 2. right, 3. right, 4. write, 5. right, 6. write, 7. right, 8. right, 9. write, 10. right

Page 95

1. to, 2. two, 3. to, 4. to, 5. too, 6. two, 7. too, 8. too, 9. to, 10. to, 11. two

Page 96

1. their, 2. They're, 3. there, 4. their, 5. there, 6. They're, 7. They're, 8. there, 9. there, 10. Their, 11. there, 12. They're

Page 97

1. sunglasses, 2. afternoon, 3. playground, 4. birthday, 5. outside, 6. scrapbook, 7. sunglasses, 8. afternoon, 9. scrapbook, 10. birthday, 11. outside, 12. playground

Page 98

1. snowball, 2. railroad, 3. rainbow, 4. sailboat, 5. jumpsuit, 6. earring, 7. airplane, 8.–10. Answers will vary.

Page 99

1. unable; not able, 2. reopened; opened again, 3. unlucky; not lucky, 4. unfair; not fair, 5. unhappy; not happy, 6. rewind; wind again, 7. rewashed; washed again, 8. uneven; not even, 9. refilled; filled again, 10. reknitted; knitted again

Page 100

1. careful; full of care, 2. harmless; without harm, 3. breakable; able to be broken, 4. dreadful; full of dread, 5. hopeful; full of hope, 6. thankful; full of thanks

Unit 5

Page 101

Answers will vary.

Page 102

1. My sister (circled) sings (underlined); 2. My brother (circled) dances (underlined); 3. They (circled) perform (underlined); 4. People (circled) clap (underlined); 5.–8. Answers will vary.

Page 103

Answers will vary. Sentences should be about school safety.

Page 104

1. Uncle Joe is a funny man., **2.** Dad told us a funny story about his dog., **3.** Firefighters are brave people.

Page 105

1. Making pasta is easy. **2.** My mom is a very busy person. **3.** Having a dog is fun, but it is also a lot of work.

Page 106

1.–3. The first sentence in each paragraph should be circled. The remaining sentences should be underlined.

Page 107

1.–3. The first sentence in each paragraph should be circled. The other sentences should be underlined.

Page 108

Top: 3, 2, 4, 1; Bottom: 2, 3, 4, 1

Page 109

Top: 4, 1, 3, 2; Bottom: 3, 2, 4, 1

Page 110

1. The story takes place at the zoo., **2.** They watch the monkeys play., **3.** They feed the seals.

Page 111

Answers will vary.

Page 112

1. The poem is about things the writer likes., **2.** Answers will vary: bows, rose, toes, nose., **3.** Answers will vary: white, blue, sweet, red, crunchy, wet, black.

Page 113

Answers will vary.

Page 114

1. birds in the writer's backyard., **2.** red, tiny, sweetly, buzz, **3.** Sentences will vary. Be sure that the sentence supports the topic.

Page 115

Answers will vary.

Page 116

1. her grandmother, **2.** to thank her grandmother

Page 117

Letters will vary. Check that the parts are all correct.

Page 118

Check that the envelope is filled in correctly.

Page 119

1. how to make a bird feeder, **2.** a pine cone, string, peanut butter, and birdseed

Page 120

Order of steps: **1.** Here is how to water a plant. **2.** First, get a watering can. **3.** Next, fill the can with water. **4.** Last, water the plant. Paragraphs will vary.

Page 121

1. Many African American people celebrate Kwanzaa., **2.** Answers will vary but should be any sentence in the paragraph except the first.

Page 122

Answers will vary.

Page 123

1. The Koala, **2.** Anita Best, **3.** that it is a good book

Page 124

Reports will vary.

Page 125

1. that a lizard should be the class pet, **2.** Answers will vary. A lizard is small and easy to care for. A lizard doesn't eat much food. A lizard is interesting to watch., **3.** vote for the lizard

Page 126

Reports will vary.

Unit 6

Page 127

1. 2, 1, 3; air, bat, cat, **2.** 3, 2, 1; rock, sea, top, **3.** 2, 3, 1; dog, egg, fish, **4.** 2, 3, 1; gate, hat, ice, **5.** 1, 3, 2; joke, king, lake, **6.** 2, 3, 1; mail, neck, owl, **7.** 2, 3, 1; walk, yes, zoo; **8.** 3, 2, 1; nail, oak, pan

Page 128

1. 3, 1, 2; hat, hill, hop; **2.** 3, 2, 1; far, four, fun; **3.** 1, 2, 3; ten, top, train; **4.** 1, 3, 2; art, ate, awful; **5.** 3, 1, 2; back, bring, bug; **6.** 2, 1, 3; gate, goat, great; **7.** 2, 1, 3; sad, snake, star; **8.** 2, 1, 3; pig, plane, prince

Page 129

1. music, noise, poem, **2.** plant, rain, sun, **3.** frog, garden, ground, **4.** afraid, alone, asleep

Page 130

1. tiny, **2.** no, **3.** toad, **4.** tiny, **5.** yes, because the word together falls between tiny and total in ABC order.

Page 131

1. burst, **2.** Grandfather and I burst into laughter., **3.** bump, **4.** 2, **5.** Answers will vary; examples: I have a bump on my head., The water pipe burst.

Page 132

1. no, **2.** no, **3.** yes, **4.** no, **5.** yes, **6.** no, **7.** no, **8.** no

Page 133

1. 8, **2.** 4, **3.** 10, **4.** 3, **5.** 11, **6.** 4, **7.** butterflies, **8.** dogs, **9.** trees or United States, **10.** history, Florida

Page 134

1. Kinds of Houses, **2.** Jack Builder, **3.** 4, **4.** page 15, **5.** 2, 9

Page 135

1. All About Cats, **2.** Patricia L. Keller, **3.** Richard H. Green, **4.** Coaster Press

Page 136

1. 5, **2.** 1, **3.** 7, **4.** "Cats in the Wild"

Page 137

1. fiction, **2.** nonfiction, **3.** nonfiction, **4.** fiction, **5.** fiction, **6.** nonfiction, **7.** fiction

Page 138

1. nonfiction, **2.** fiction, **3.** nonfiction, **4.** fiction, **5.–8.** Answers will vary.

Page 139

1. fact, **2.** fantasy, **3.** fantasy, **4.** fact, **5.** fantasy, **6.** fantasy, **7.** fact, **8.** fantasy

Page 140

1. fantasy, **2.** fact, **3.** fact, **4.** fantasy, **5.** fact, **6.** fact **7.** fantasy, **8.** fact